T0301976

"An essential read for grasping and harnessing the competitive advantages, collaborative strength, and positive societal influence wielded by SMEs. This book covers, in particular, the concept of "future readiness" which should be part of any business strategy in today's volatile world, especially for SMEs."

Julia Devos
Head, New Champions Community
World Economic Forum

"This book serves an important goal by introducing its reader to the sustainability challenges faced by SMEs, who play a big role in society by employing a significant chunk of human capital. The book delves into important topics, such as the role of technology in shaping our economic landscape through the reshaping of SMEs and how effective change management can be brought to help SMEs manage changes permeating throughout the world. This book is a recommended read for students of the global business environment, as our world stands at the intersection of technological advancement and sustainability challenges, and SMEs are expected to play a crucial role in navigating these challenges."

Rohit Nishant
Professor of Information Systems
Queen's University, Belfast

"Rajah's work effectively highlights the need for companies to shift from a reactive to a more proactive approach. This is a crucial aspect of building future readiness, especially for SMEs that have the advantage of agility but are often constrained by their size and resources. The simple framework and practical examples provided along the three core axes of sustainability, technology, and talent are valuable and offer SME leaders cross-cutting keys to develop a more future-oriented approach. This will not only benefit individual businesses but also society as a whole."

Olivier Woeffray
Foresight, Strategy and Insights Lead
Arup

The Biggest Winners are Small

are Small

Understanding
Sustainability and Future
Readiness of Global
Small and Medium-Sized
Enterprises

The Biggest Winners are Small

Understanding Sustainability and Future Readiness of Global Small and Medium-Sized Enterprises

Rashimah Rajah

University of Twente, the Netherlands

World Scientific

NEW JERSEY · LONDON · SINGAPORE · BEIJING · SHANGHAI · HONG KONG · TAIPEI · CHENNAI · TOKYO

Published by

World Scientific Publishing Co. Pte. Ltd.

5 Toh Tuck Link, Singapore 596224

USA office: 27 Warren Street, Suite 401-402, Hackensack, NJ 07601

UK office: 57 Shelton Street, Covent Garden, London WC2H 9HE

Library of Congress Cataloging-in-Publication Data

Names: Rajah, Rashimah, author.

Title: The biggest winners are small : understanding sustainability and future readiness of global
small and medium-sized enterprises / Rashimah Rajah, University of Twente, the Netherlands.

Description: New Jersey : World Scientific, [2024] | Includes bibliographical references and index.

Identifiers: LCCN 2024017627 | ISBN 9789811293740 (hardcover) |
ISBN 9789811293757 (ebook) | ISBN 9789811293764 (ebook other)

Subjects: LCSH: Small business. | Sustainable development.

Classification: LCC HD2341 .R34 2024 | DDC 338.6/42--dc23/eng/20240419

LC record available at https://lccn.loc.gov/2024017627

British Library Cataloguing-in-Publication Data

A catalogue record for this book is available from the British Library.

For any available supplementary material, please visit
https://www.worldscientific.com/worldscibooks/10.1142/13855#t=suppl

Desk Editors: Sanjay Varadharajan/Kura Sunaina

Typeset by Stallion Press
Email: enquiries@stallionpress.com

Printed in Singapore

Preface

If there is one thing I can say for certain, it is that life as we know it is becoming increasingly uncertain. It sounds cliché, but it is true. Change is the only constant, and in today's environment, changes glare at you in your face. In the past, the powerful and mighty could try to prevent change, or have more control of changes happening in the environment, but now, the tables have turned. Those who are most flexible and nimble stand to gain the most from the changes occurring, and it is no longer the large and mighty corporations that necessarily have the advantage. It is the small companies that are gaining the competitive edge — those that adapt quickly to changes in the market environment and those that are brave enough to seize opportunities when others see a crisis.

This book highlights the power that small and medium-sized enterprises (SMEs) have in staying competitive and overcoming the obstacles of the future. Despite making up more than 90% of all businesses, SMEs have traditionally been overlooked as an influential driver for positive change. This book highlights the importance of sustainability and future readiness in companies, and places the spotlight on this previously overlooked segment of the economy.

From analyzing business operations and business models to understanding the role of technology to highlighting the importance of the human touch, this book covers multiple aspects of an organization and acts as an introductory guide to those who wish to have a better understanding of future readiness.

Featuring case study companies from which we all can draw best practices from, I highlight some practical recommendations on how founders and decision makers in SMEs can lead their company to future readiness. I am constantly inspired by the courage and tenacity displayed by the SME "underdogs". My hope is that through this book, you will be inspired, too.

About the Author

Rashimah Rajah is Assistant Professor of Organizational Behavior and Technology at the University of Twente in the Netherlands. Having had appointments previously at the National University of Singapore, Koblenz University of Applied Sciences in Germany, Coastal Carolina University in the USA, and Brock University in Canada, Rashimah brings a myriad of international experiences and perspectives into researching organizational behavior.

Photo: Susanne Dröppelmann

Rashimah is an Academic Expert with the World Economic Forum, lending her expertise as a panelist, for instance, at the New Champions Retreat in Geneva. She has published in *Leadership Quarterly, Ivey Business Publishing*, and *Handbook of Research on Crisis Leadership in Organizations*, among others, on leadership and technology. This book — *The Biggest Winners are Small* — expresses her passion for research in leadership and technology in the context of SMEs.

Rashimah obtained her Ph.D. in Management and Organization from the prestigious National University of Singapore under the President Graduate Fellowship. She regularly contributes to news commentaries and provides interviews on research topics, with her insights published in *Channel NewsAsia, South China Morning Post*, and *The Business Times*.

Contents

Acknowledgments

I would like to thank my collaborators at the World Economic Forum, as well as my colleagues at the National University of Singapore, especially Siok Tambyah, for your support in bouncing off ideas, reading drafts of the chapters, and providing valuable input and feedback for various portions of the book. I appreciate our collegiality and I am thankful to be called your colleague and your friend.

I would also like to thank the multiple founders, CEOs, and executive decision makers who have graciously allowed me to feature your fantastic companies in this book as an inspiration to others: Sheraan Amod, Esther An, Sriram Bharatam, Stanislas Bocquet, Brendon Boyce, Magda Chelly, Jessica JJ Chuan, Jay Huang, Erik Ingvoldstad, and Sandra Nguyen Si.

Thanks also to the publishers for their grace and invaluable support.

Lastly and most importantly, I would like to thank my mom and dad, without whom I would be literally nothing.

Part One

Introduction

Chapter 1
Predictably Unpredictable

Climate change, a global pandemic, the Great Resignation wave, ongoing wars, hyperinflation, supply chain disruptions, and the rapid rise of artificial intelligence (AI). If the past few years have taught us anything, it is that the only thing we can predict is that the future is unpredictable. In one moment, the technology sector is a safe bet, and in the next, the tech sector is seeing hundreds of thousands of layoffs. Companies which started being wary of AI and banned innovations like ChatGPT now embrace AI and are learning to optimize business operations using machine learning algorithms.

Change is happening so quickly that I am almost certain that between the time this book is published and when it reaches the reader's hands (or device), new global events will take place, figures will be updated, new trends as well as new threats will be taken into account in business decisions, and we might also see some trends turning in the opposite direction. I am experiencing that as an instructor in the university — ChatGPT was banned in my class assignments just one semester ago because students should respect intellectual property and not pass off the work of someone else — even if there is no "author" in ChatGPT in the traditional sense — as their own. ChatGPT produces well-written work with (mostly) reliable sources, so it is tempting for students to copy and paste the output wholesale. Now, I openly allow students to use AI.

I encourage students to use ChatGPT to get basic explanations of and understand management concepts that we learn in class, and to improve on it with their personal insights and reflection. In other words, instead of being fearful of the negative consequences that technology could bring to the classroom learning, I embraced this change and leveraged it to improve learning, encouraging students to dig that much deeper to produce something that reflects more profound insight. Inadvertently, the learning standards for everyone increased. Students expect me as an instructor to go beyond mere explanation of management concepts — they can find that out on their own — and I expect students to do more than regurgitate definitions in their assignments. Basic rules still apply: Students must still credit the work that they did not create themselves, even if that credit now goes to a machine.

Despite the unpredictability of the future, we should still equip ourselves with as much information as possible moving forward. There is no doubt that a tinge (or even huge amounts) of agility is required to tweak our decisions along the way to fit the evolving environment. In this book, we will examine elements of an organization that allow a business to be better prepared for the rapid changes of the future. This book will focus on the **future readiness** of businesses, and management decisions that increase the future readiness levels of companies. In particular, this book will focus on the future readiness of small and medium-sized enterprises (SMEs).

Why SMEs?

Much attention in books and case studies has been focused on large organizations and their strategies in having the edge in business environments — and rightly so. They create 40% of jobs globally,[1] invest heavily in research and development (R&D) to introduce some of the most advanced technological innovations to the market, have enough power to collaborate with governmental bodies to shape local regulations, and can also bring transfer of knowledge, technology, and infrastructure to less-developed countries. Multinational corporations (MNCs) attract foreign direct investments and allow host economies to integrate into and upgrade global value chains.

However, despite the large impact of MNCs, the reality is that more than 90% of all businesses are SMEs. There are different estimates regarding the impact SMEs have on employment. The World Bank estimated that SMEs make up for about 50% of employment worldwide,[2] and the International Labor Organization reported that SMEs can account for up to 70% of employment and global GDP.[3] According to OECD statistics, some countries such as Canada, South Korea, and China have more than 80% of their private sector employees working in SMEs.[4] Clearly, SMEs have a massive collective impact. However, for a long time, this group of companies has largely been overlooked.

Definition of SMEs

SMEs are typically defined by the number of full-time employees in the organization. A company is categorized as small if it employs between 10 and 49 full-time employees. A medium-sized enterprise employs between 50 and 250 full-time employees. Recently, the term "mid-sized" has been introduced to acknowledge a category of businesses that is located in the space between SMEs and large corporations. A mid-sized company employs fewer than 4,999 full-time employees and its turnover does not exceed US$1.75 billion. Some case study companies in this book are identified in the "mid-sized" category. However, their featured stories stem from when they were smaller in size. Also, the changing nature of businesses today has blurred the relationships between size and revenue. For example, "unicorns", or start-ups with a valuation of over US$1 billion, typically start small.

As the changing world pushes us to rethink the way we work and conduct our day-to-day activities, SMEs are increasingly in the spotlight. For example, the COVID-19 pandemic amplified the need for businesses to be agile and adaptable to remain viable. Local and global restrictions during the pandemic meant that important supply chains were disrupted, sectors reliant on physical work such as manufacturing and construction shut down temporarily, and the nature of customer interactions changed for good. However, what the world saw as a complete overturn is what small companies have called their way of life.

Even prior to the global health emergency, small companies needed to be agile. Small companies which had insufficient finances to rent office spaces, for instance, have always encouraged working from home (or working from anywhere) and leveraged technological platforms such as Slack, Google Meets, and Mira to collaborate on organizational tasks. Due to the unpredictable nature of the market environment for many small companies, leaders and employees have been used to adapting to evolving needs, such as rebranding their product, or coming up with creative solutions to achieve set outcomes and deliver to clients. Recent global events have only emphasized how important adaptability and agility are — strengths already inherent in SMEs.

Admittedly, SMEs have been among the hardest hit by turbulences and shocks in the local and global market environment. The following are some impacts of the COVID-19 crisis. A study in China found that 18% of SMEs closed for good between February and May 2020, shedding 14% of total jobs.[5] SMEs in London, which account for 48% of total business turnover, were severely affected, with 28% of SME employees being furloughed. The greatest hit was the accommodation and food sector, with 71% of employees furloughed.[6] Compared to big companies with more resources to keep operations running remotely and workers employed, SMEs were affected through dismissals and hiring freezes as they cut costs and looked to simply survive.

However, SMEs were also among the biggest winners of COVID-19. Nimbler to integrate and produce innovations such as AI and deep learning, big data, the Internet of Things, and green technologies, SMEs came out on top as they harnessed the power of disruptive technology to keep up with the rapid changes, with strategies executed quickly and flexibly. In facing the uncertainties of the future, SMEs were on the one hand most vulnerable, but on the other hand possessed the highest advantage in being able to pivot. They were, and still are, in the best position to reallocate their resources for a more suitable strategy and leverage digital technologies to scale at lower cost.

Some examples of these companies will be illustrated in this book. However, a quick look at CNBC's annual Disruptor 50 lists from 2013 to 2023 will show us that it is the smaller companies that are at the epicenter of market-changing innovations. Many of the companies on the Disruptor 50 list in 2020 are unicorns that have already reached or passed the $1 billion valuation mark. More impressively, they *grew* since the pandemic began. 74% of them hired new employees and 38% successfully pivoted their products or launched new ones to meet the challenges of the pandemic.[7] They are also among the more progressive companies in diversity, equity, and inclusion. 13 of 2023's Disruptors have a female founder and 14 of them feature CEOs from racial and ethnic minorities.[8]

Clearly, there is much potential in SMEs in furthering the global agenda of innovation and sustainability. Given that more than 90% of all companies are SMEs, there is much power to be held if recipes for success can be replicated across industries and regions. That is one objective of this book. It aims to provide some clarity in a world of unpredictability. With this book, founders do not necessarily have to solve all challenges as if they are being confronted with them for the first time. They can have an understanding of levers of future readiness and recognize which lever to pull to give them a better chance of dealing with the risks of the future.

There are best practices from what we call "Future-Ready SMEs" for founders and decision makers to draw inspiration from. Depending on their size, industry, geographical location, and current state of digital infrastructure, SMEs can understand from their peers *how* they can contribute to future-ready goals in their space *while* pursuing profitability. Ultimately, there is still an element of trial and error in implementing any kind of strategy in smaller businesses. However, by identifying several core elements of future-ready SMEs rooted in vision, leadership, and technology, among others, I hope to give readers a sense of what they should prioritize to future-proof their company.

Outline

This book is divided into five parts:

1. **Introduction**: In this part, we look at SMEs in the context of the global economy and highlight their importance in driving innovation and future readiness. SMEs stand to be the biggest winners in our current market conditions, where size — previously perceived as a liability — now lends a competitive advantage to companies to survive and thrive in a volatile, uncertain, complex, and ambiguous (VUCA) environment.

2. **Understanding Future Readiness**: In the second part of this book, I present the definition of future readiness and a nomological network of drivers and pillars of future readiness. I also share findings of a global assessment of SMEs in researching future readiness. We look at industrial and regional aspects which may affect SMEs' levels of future readiness, and test the nomological network empirically. In discussing future readiness, we highlight that sustainability or societal impact is a huge factor. In line with environmental, social, and governance (ESG) goals, SMEs should understand that sustainability is no longer a "good-to-have" element

outside of the business model, but should be heavily considered in both the input and output decisions of the business. While there will naturally be new factors or developments in the field that impact this model in the future, I posit that it is comprehensive enough to cover new trends or contexts which may be subsumed into one or more of the factors presented. For example, a new technological trend with a different name can still be subsumed in the "digital infrastructure" aspect of the model.

3. **Challenges in the Market Environment**: The third part of this book highlights the challenges presented by the market environment that SMEs need to keep up with. In particular, this part discusses sustainability and technology, with case studies featured to show how smaller companies meet these demands and stay ahead of their competitors.

4. **People as an Asset**: In the fourth part, we examine people as a crucial resource for SMEs and discuss talent and leadership to highlight the human aspect in driving future readiness of smaller companies. As the famous quote goes, "Culture eats strategy for breakfast." For SMEs, people and culture are on the table for breakfast, lunch, and dinner.

5. **Change Management**: In the last part of this book, we go through the principles of change management and elucidate the different strategies that SMEs might choose to pursue compared to bigger multinationals, as they continue on, or pivot to, the path of future readiness. Drawing from a mix of classic and contemporary theories on change management, we highlight the biggest barriers to change and offer several possible ways to overcome them.

Who This Book Is Meant For

This book covers general management topics and is meant for academics, practitioners, and graduate (MBA) students as a starting point to understand (i) the significance of SMEs in driving the global economy and sustainability agenda, (ii) drivers and pillars of future readiness, and (iii) best practices of companies featured in case studies in achieving high levels of future readiness. Although this book is meant as an introductory book to SMEs' future readiness, some prior knowledge on general management and organizational behavior might be useful.

There may be an overlap between chapters because of the iterative nature of management in businesses. For example, when there is effective leadership, a conducive environment can be created in the company which can spur innovation. This type of environment could attract the right type of talent for the organization who will work hard to achieve a common goal. When the workforce is reliable and operates smoothly on its own, resources are freed up for the leader to pursue other organizational goals, such as to secure funding and capital for the company. This in turn benefits employees of the organization through more resources which allow them to innovate, investment in technologies which support the company's digital transformation, and a more positive organizational climate. The cycle continues as *these* factors in the organization make it more attractive for investors to trust the founder with their investment.

Depending on the stage of one's business, or one's preexisting knowledge, some chapters may be more relevant than others. This simulates decision-making in the real world where priorities need to be made. For instance, while a company could attempt to pursue a maximum level of future readiness by executing as many strategies as possible, the reality is that companies need to prioritize their strategies. This is especially the case for SMEs, known for their limited resources. While there exist multiple levers to pull, what we hope to show in this book is that it is possible to work on one particular aspect of the business strategy to achieve multiple goals for future readiness.

Ultimately, what is important is to realize that change is inevitable. To succeed, we need to embrace change, be adaptable, and enjoy the process. **Life is a rollercoaster: Those who thrive the most are those who enjoy the ride**.

Part Two

Understanding
Future Readiness

Chapter 2

Nomological Network of Future Readiness

What Is Future Readiness?

To guide us in having a common understanding of "future readiness" throughout this book, it is best to provide a definition for this term. Future readiness refers to the extent to which companies successfully respond to external factors which may disrupt their operations. It also involves organizations' successful ability to seize opportunities that emerge from such disruptions. Future-ready companies integrate considerations based on present and future trends, threats, and opportunities into their business model. The focus is on long-term growth and survival, as these companies are also conscious of the impact that they have on society and the environment.

Outcomes of future readiness consist of three pillars: (i) long-term growth, (ii) societal impact, and (iii) adaptive capacity.[1] In each of these pillars, a balance between immediate and future needs is present. Long-term growth takes into account *both* financial performance of a company and its level of innovation compared to its competitors. The idea is that companies which exhibit long-term growth create financial value through innovative business models, products, and/or services.

Societal impact refers to a company's positive outcomes for the environment and society, as the business model addresses positive and negative potential externalities. Companies which generate positive societal impact engage in activities in pursuit of sustainability goals for the greater good, such as having an explicit vision and mission statement aimed at sustainability, and offering products and/or services that positively benefit the environment and community. Adaptive capacity involves two seemingly opposite forces. First, it requires high levels of organizational resilience such that the company can absorb shocks or externalities to remain viable. Second, it encapsulates high levels of agility where the company then adapts and seizes opportunities with an evolving market.

Long-Term Growth

Decision makers of small and medium-sized enterprises are famously — or infamously — in constant "firefighting mode". Access to funding and capital remains a large concern for executives as they have obligations to compensate their employees, pay overheads, invest in tools and technologies for the business, and overall, keep the company alive. Many SMEs are dependent on their current "traditional" business model to generate profits. With low cash reserves, deviating from a business recipe that works could spell financial trouble, rendering them unable to continue their operations.

However, future-ready companies recognize that it is *through* innovation that the company can continue generating financial value. In a fast-changing market environment, companies which stay ahead of the competition are those that are able to provide clients with unique products and/or services, develop revolutionary marketing programs, and adopt the latest technology in their industry. For example, Levven, a medium-sized enterprise from Canada, leverages the Internet of Things (IoT) to develop home automation products. This includes producing wireless switches which control lighting in the house. This innovation not only brings wireless automation to the construction industry but also requires fewer raw materials to make traditional switches (copper, plastic, and metal screws), which translates into waste reduction and savings passed on to consumers. Indeed, due to Levven's innovation, homes have become more affordable for individuals, couples, and families. This gain in customer traction naturally allows Levven's financial profits to grow.

Societal Impact

A by-product of Levven's innovation is a positive impact on the environment. Homes become more sustainable through waste reduction — Levven's innovation conserves 35% of the electrical wire at construction — and automation features in switches help to maximize power savings.[2] This brings us to the second pillar of future readiness: societal impact. For the purpose of

this book, societal impact and sustainability are used interchangeably. Sustainability refers to the ability of an organization's ecosystem to continue functioning into the indefinite future without being forced into decline through the exhaustion or overloading of key resources on which that system depends. Here, a company takes into consideration environmental and social factors in its performance and strategy.

Societal impact is measured by the extent to which companies pursue sustainable goals by developing specific outcome indicators to measure their positive contributions to the global sustainability agenda. One useful framework is the United Nations' 17 Sustainable Development Goals (SDGs). Companies ranked high on the societal impact dimension of future readiness are those that pursue these SDGs by having a written mission statement that includes an explicit commitment to positive social and/or environmental impact, have dedicated staff to oversee sustainability issues, have formal processes to incorporate social and/or environmental considerations in the business strategy of the company, and have senior leadership involved in approving policies related to sustainability.

Adaptive Capacity

Adaptive capacity somewhat represents a two-step process. A company with high adaptive capacity needs to be resilient enough to absorb disruptions to its business *and* also be agile enough to quickly and easily respond to changes in the external environment to provide a new or revised offering to the market. In an ideal scenario, a company with high adaptive capacity could turn a crisis into an opportunity. For example, RecoMed, an online healthcare booking platform and marketplace in South Africa, seized the opportunities presented by the global crisis of the COVID-19 pandemic. RecoMed connects practitioners, patients, and other stakeholders in the healthcare ecosystem. Keen to offer patients ease of booking appointments with a trusted and diverse selection of healthcare providers quickly and privately, this small enterprise leverages proprietary API-based deep industry integrations to provide advanced patient–practitioner interfaces. RecoMed's marketplace also connects healthcare providers directly to a variety of medical schemes, life insurers, websites, and other channels that drive increased patient footfall into their practices.

When the COVID-19 pandemic began in early 2020, South Africa entered a national lockdown, preventing patients from physically visiting doctors for non-critical care. RecoMed responded by designing a virtual consultation telehealth system integrated with its core platform, thereby allowing consumers to book virtual consultations with doctors. RecoMed engaged Amazon Web Services for assistance and ultimately implemented its proprietary video streaming technology service called Chime into a final RecoMed virtual consultation product. Upon the launch of this product in June 2020, several key partners of RecoMed adopted the company's telehealth solution.[3] With telehealth bookings rapidly adopted by practitioners nationwide, it now contributes toward the 100,000+ healthcare bookings per month powered by RecoMed.

According to CEO and founder Sheraan Amod, "A technology company should be ready to adapt almost instantly to shifting market forces, and there was no greater sudden shift than when COVID-19 appeared. Fortunately, the direction of innovation was clearly future-focused as telehealth was inevitable due to its convenience appeal. However, COVID-19 played a material role in

---

Resilience in SMEs

For a company to be able to buffer the negative impacts of a shock or crisis, it needs to ensure that it has enough financial and non-financial (e.g., human) resources. These resources, also termed as slack resources, tend to be lacking in SMEs. Smaller companies possess fewer cash reserves and manpower to keep operations running as smoothly as they did before the crisis. Later in this book, we will discuss how future-ready SMEs *redefine* organizational resilience. Through the numerous interviews and discussions with CEOs and founders of SMEs featured in this book, a common theme that arises is that companies gain its resilience not by relying on the amount of resources they have, but on the *quality* of these resources. In particular, future-ready SMEs cite their *people* as the main ingredient in building organizational resilience. A resilient people and a resilient mindset help circumvent SMEs' lack of access to more traditional forms of slack resources.

hastening its adoption." With the trend of telehealth consultations seeming to be more permanent moving forward, RecoMed exhibited high adaptive capacity as it quickly seized a tremendous opportunity from a crisis situation.

Future Readiness as a Composite of Its Three Pillars

Admittedly, there are overlaps in the three dimensions of future readiness. A profit-generating innovation can simultaneously pursue sustainability goals. This innovation can also be a result of the organization's high adaptive capacity. Nonetheless, understanding future readiness based on these three pillars still provides us with a useful frame from which companies can assess their own levels of future readiness. This is particularly important for SMEs which tend to lack internal resources to conduct detailed assessments carried out by experts. By understanding the different dimensions of future readiness, SMEs could identify gaps present in their business model and make necessary modifications to be more future-ready.

For instance, if a company is high on innovation, but societal impact does not represent one of the objectives of the organization, it may find itself unable to survive in the future in light of concerns and preferences for more sustainable products and services. Investors are also increasingly looking at impact investing or green investments, and the rising importance of environmental, social, and governance (ESG) investments may soon provide us with standardized metrics upon which companies are measured. SMEs which do not address gaps in future readiness may find themselves losing out not only to bigger companies — which may have had more resources to start on their sustainability efforts sooner — but also to their competitors that are coming up with creative ways to pursue the dual goals of sustainability and profit, as in the earlier example of Levven. Besides, companies also need to keep up with changing legislations. The European Union (EU), for instance, has a target of a 100% reduction in EU fleet-wide carbon dioxide emission for cars and vans from 2035 onward.[4] Automotive companies which innovate without societal impact considerations will face significant challenges in light of updated standards.

To be "truly" future-ready, companies should strive for high levels on all three pillars of future readiness. Identifying a specific pillar of future readiness in which the company is lacking can provide a starting point for SME executives in deciding if they should invest in more resources to make up for their weaknesses, or to lean into their strengths. RecoMed, for instance, identifies itself primarily as a technology company and leaned into its technical expertise to launch its new offering on its platform.

To assess where they stand in terms of future readiness, SMEs can analyze their business operations based on whether they are pursuing long-term growth, consciously making a positive societal impact, or ensuring that they can be resilient and agile to pivot when the situation requires it. There are also self-assessment tools, such as one at the World Economic Forum website,[a] which utilizes established measures of future readiness.

What is important to recognize is that the external environment is dynamic and SMEs need to reevaluate their future readiness at regular intervals, taking into account trends in the market, legislative changes, geopolitical issues, and global events. While a company vision should be stable, business models or strategies should be reviewed more frequently. Companies can look to industry standards or create their own standards with regard to the frequency of these reevaluations of their future readiness levels. PALO IT, for instance, a tech consultancy firm, conducts reassessments every 6 months.

Antecedents or Drivers of Future Readiness

The following is the nomological network for future readiness, where we identify the antecedents or the drivers of the three pillars of future readiness (Figure 1). A company is divided into "Power of the People" and "Business Operations", addressing the importance of the interaction between structural factors of an organization and the human touch. Under Business Operations, the factors that drive future readiness are business orientation, business model, networks, governance, and digital infrastructure. Under Power of the People, the model highlights the importance of authentic leadership and talent fit to run business operations efficiently.

---

[a] The self-assessment tool on the website also offers instant reports showing where a company ranks on the different aspects of future readiness compared to its competitors.

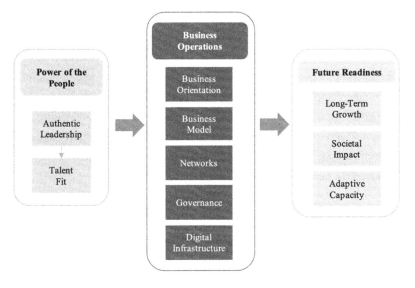

Figure 1. Nomological network of future readiness.

Business Orientation

Orientation refers to the culture or style of an organization that defines the ways in which it deals with important decisions. There are five sub-dimensions of business orientation: (i) autonomy, which refers to the extent of freedom given to employees to make important decisions independently, (ii) innovativeness,[b] the inclination of companies to support new ideas and experimentation, (iii) proactiveness, which is the ability to anticipate and pursue new opportunities in the market, (iv) risk-taking, the tendency for companies to take action despite incomplete information or predicted likelihood of failure, and (v) competitive aggressiveness, which refers to the ability to challenge competitors to gain entry or improve the company's current market position.

Different combinations of the five sub-dimensions are possible, depending on the types of opportunities that companies pursue. For instance, risk-taking

---

[b] This is not to be confused with "innovation". Innovation refers to a novel method, product, or idea which aids in value creation. Innovativeness refers to the process or culture within the company that encourages innovation, and may not necessarily lead to the innovation.

can range from low nominal-level risks (such as depositing money in a bank or restocking shelves) to "high"-risk activities (such as heavy borrowing or investing in unexplored technologies).[5] Companies with high business orientation embed systems and processes to create a culture desirable for growth and innovation. For instance, employees are rewarded for having the courage to share new ideas and performance appraisals are centered on employees' ability to identify and act on new opportunities for the business. In turn, managers should provide an environment safe for risk-taking and experimentation, and should not punish employees for failures during this process.

Business Model

The business model of a company describes how an organization generates, delivers, and captures value. Included in the business model are the vision of the company, identification of its consumer base, and sources of revenue. While a vision of the company should be stable as highlighted earlier — Levven's vision, for example, is to make homes more affordable and sustainable — the *way* in which a company can reach that vision could be flexible.

We showcase in this book various examples on how the *visions* of future-ready companies are independent of technology and short-term changes in the market. However, companies with high levels of future readiness are able to redesign their chains of resources, reuse or adapt existing resources for other purposes, and integrate new information into their strategic plan based on ongoing changes in internal or external circumstances, i.e., have high business model flexibility.[c] While parts of a business model need to be stable to leverage a company's strength and expertise, other aspects must be flexible, as the strategy is refined to better cope with new challenges presented by the market.

Networks

Networks refer to systems of formal and informal professional relationships, where members mutually support efforts to increase the effectiveness of their

---

[c] Business model flexibility is not to be mixed up with the agility dimension of adaptive capacity. Business model flexibility refers to an organization's *capabilities* to be flexible in order to respond to changing demands of the market. Agility refers to the actual (quick) response to the changes in the environment (e.g., consumer demands, competitors, and/or new regional or international markets).

business activities. Understood as the microprocesses that organizations engage in to connect people in their social network either by introducing disconnected individuals or facilitating new coordination between connected individuals,[6] networks provide access and opportunities in the form of financial, social, and information resources. Learning opportunities through the sharing of knowledge and expertise with partners, as well as through engagement with learning and development activities in their supply networks, encourage the processes of innovation and continuous improvement.

Based on practical insights collected from various decision makers in SMEs, networks can come in the form of (i) peers and the intelligence individuals can gather from exchanging information with each other, (ii) ties with the government and policy makers, whose decisions at the local and national level shape the environment SMEs are in, and (iii) affiliation with foundations and larger networks like the United Nations and non-governmental organizations. Networks are especially important for companies which are starting out. Accounts from interviews with various founders show the need for them to tap into their professional and personal networks to access financial and non-financial resources at the beginning. Not only is networking important to overcome the initial barriers related to trust but it also provides access to diverse skill sets and expertise needed by the company.

Coming back to the example of Levven, CEO James Keirstead reached out to service providers in the affiliations he belonged to, Entrepreneurs' Organization (EO), and Startup Edmonton (now a program of Edmonton Unlimited) to connect with different communities in the technology and entrepreneurial space. Connecting to others in the tech community not only helped Levven get the technical help it needed but it also aided in increasing the credibility of the company in the ecosystem. Networking helped Levven build and grow its connections to the point that now, it is others who are approaching the company, and not the other way around. Compared to larger corporations, networks represent an extremely important aspect for SMEs.

It is important to note here that mere connection to networks or affiliation to influential bodies does not necessarily lend smaller companies a competitive advantage. These networks need to be relevant in furthering the organization's goals, be diverse, and utilize "structural holes" (Figure 2). A structural hole refers to a gap between two individuals in a network that represents

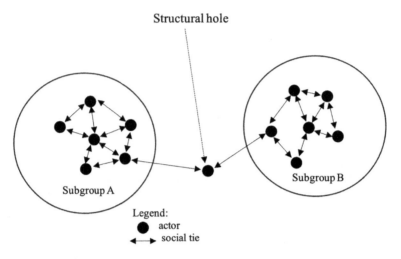

Figure 2. Illustration of a structural hole in connecting two subgroups of networks.

complementary skill sets or knowledge.[7] Additionally, research posits that *weak ties* could benefit individuals more than strong ones. It is the idea that acquaintances, rather than close partners, are more advantageous, as connections to people outside of one's central network act as bridges to other groups of people, subsequently creating a more diverse network and access to a larger pool of resources.[8]

With developments in communications technology and the advent of social media, it is now easier for business owners to reach out to a greater global network in a short amount of time. Although trust-building may take a longer time as virtual introductions — as opposed to face-to-face ones — are becoming the norm, entrepreneurs who leverage these networks can stand to reap the benefits associated with traditional physical networking events. However, they need to be cognizant that additional effort is required to overcome communication barriers[d] in order to form high-quality relationships.

---

[d] According to media richness theory, virtual communication through emails and text messages represents a less rich form of communication. This can lead to miscommunication as the lack of body language and potential language differences may mean that the intended tone is not properly conveyed through these messages.

Governance

Increasingly, there is focus on ESG (environmental, social, and governance) aspects in measuring companies' sustainability efforts. While the "E" and "S" aspects of ESG are well covered in theory and in practice — as they are more straightforward to address — more attention needs to be placed on the "G" aspect of ESG. Governance comprises five dimensions: (i) governing purpose and strategy, (ii) quality of governing body, (iii) stakeholder engagement, (iv) ethical behavior, and (v) risk and opportunity oversight.[9] These dimensions cover theoretical aspects of governance like strategy and analysis of risks and opportunities, as well as practical aspects like ethical behavior, quality of the governing body, and stakeholder engagement.

Companies that exhibit high levels of governance engage in, among other things, (i) training members on the company's anti-corruption policies and procedures, (ii) having formal procedures to address results from stakeholder engagement, including having designated teams and/or individuals for appropriate follow-up, and (iii) having executive compensation tied to the company's social and/or environmental performance. Here, it is important to note that governance is perceived as a *precursor* to societal impact and is not to be confused with the *impact* itself.

In SMEs, governance represents something new, about which little is known. Not only do executives need to find out more about what governance exactly means and entails but lean business operations in smaller companies also mean that having dedicated staff to address governance is difficult. Often, SMEs find themselves addressing governance as an ad hoc issue (e.g., when it is requested by investors or other stakeholders), having current full-time employees deal with governance as an additional task which is not part of their original job scope, or not engaging in governance at all. With the rising importance of ESG, it is important for companies to *integrate* governance into the businesses' modus operandi to pursue increased levels of future readiness.

Digital Infrastructure

Digital infrastructure refers to an IT portfolio that a company has. This includes technologies like cloud computing, wearables, mobile technologies, social media, and business analytics. To keep up with evolving trends in regulations and in the consumer market, SMEs require sound digital infrastructure for the production or adoption of a value-added novel creation, development of new methods of production, and new management systems and business models.

Although smaller companies are less able to invest in digital technologies, the ability for small companies to leverage technology to create disruptive innovations, and to scale with relatively lower overhead costs, shows that digital infrastructure can be a catalyst for future readiness. On the topic of sustainability, companies may indeed address environmental and social concerns the "traditional way" without using technology. This includes reducing their carbon footprint non-digitally and engaging in more inclusive hiring practices. However, in this book, we show how SMEs can leverage technology to make a positive impact to society, pursuing sustainability goals while the company simultaneously makes advancements in digital technology.

Power of the People

The most important part of this model is understanding the power of the people as "meta-drivers" of future readiness. It is the people who set the tone and vision of the company, design the business strategies, and make adaptations to these strategies to remain relevant in today's competitive market. While it is important for companies to have sustainable business models and operations which "run themselves" with minimal human intervention, various roundtables and in-depth interviews with prominent decision makers of SMEs have never failed to highlight the importance of people in smaller companies. They represent the source of vision, values, and resilience. Before a company grows to be a large one with established procedures, legacy systems, and steady ways of generating value, meta-drivers in the form of leadership and employees remain crucial in small and medium-sized enterprises.

Authentic Leadership

Leaders who are clear on their vision, are able to inspire employees to collectively reach that vision, and can harness benefits from networking, are deemed to be

effective leaders in future-ready SMEs. In our nomological network, we identify **authentic leadership** to be the style that best describes the leadership that is important in driving companies' future readiness levels. Authentic leadership refers to a leadership style that includes leading with a vision and values and encouraging followers to behave authentically according to shared values.[10] Through increased self-awareness, self-regulation, and positive modeling, authentic leaders foster the development of authenticity in followers. By leading in alignment with followers' values, leaders increase follower motivation, which leads to increased productivity and organizational commitment from the employees.

Authentic leaders display (i) deep self-awareness of their strengths and limitations, (ii) a high level of transparency and openness with others which provides followers with an opportunity to be forthcoming with their ideas, challenges, and opinions, (iii) a high standard for ethical and moral conduct, and (iv) balanced processing, i.e., the leader solicits sufficient opinions and viewpoints before making important decisions.[11] Authentic leaders draw inspiration from their personal values to lead an organization as they are deeply aware of how they think and behave, and ensure that their actions are aligned with their core beliefs. Followers or employees are in turn empowered to be their authentic selves, exerting greater effort in helping the company reach its organizational goals.

Talent Fit

Talent acquisition and retention are some of the major concerns of decision makers in SMEs. Being less reputable than large conglomerates and with lower ability to attract talent using financial incentives, how can smaller companies appeal to people, who, as highlighted earlier, represent a great source of resilience and strength for the organization? The answer lies in prioritizing talent *fit*. An SME whose hiring process includes values and culture fit of candidates — as opposed to hiring purely based on technical qualifications — is in a better position to execute its future-ready business strategies. We will expound upon this in Chapter 6 in the fourth part of the book. For smaller companies, hiring the "right" people takes on an unconventional definition.

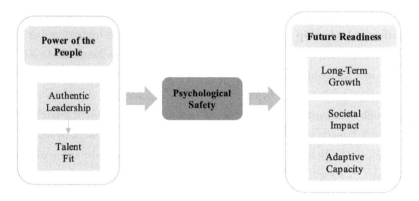

Figure 3. The role of psychological safety in future readiness.

Authentic leadership is positively related to talent fit in the company. Leaders who are authentic themselves and encourage authenticity in followers hire based on values alignment. Evidence has repeatedly shown that the "right" people are crucial in SMEs: those who believe in the company's purpose, work collaboratively with others in the company, and have the resourcefulness and passion in completing work tasks. This is indeed what sets future-ready SMEs apart from their competitors and from larger companies.

Psychological Safety as a Mediator

The process of how people (leaders and employees) drive future readiness is aided by what we call psychological safety (Figure 3). Psychological safety refers to an environment where it is safe for members of an organization to voice their ideas and opinions without judgment or consequences.[12] It refers to a culture where employees are empowered to take risks, while being able to admit mistakes and learn and progress together. With effective communication from the top management on shared values that influence the HR processes on recruitment and talent development, SMEs achieve higher long-term growth, societal impact, and adaptive capacity through psychological safety.

Now that we have outlined the nomological network of future readiness, consisting of factors particularly relevant to SMEs, we conduct a global assessment of SME future readiness in Chapter 3, based on data collected over the past years.

Chapter 3
Global Assessment of SME Future Readiness

Global Survey

The findings presented in this chapter constitute the result of a collaborative effort with the World Economic Forum (WEF). As part of the New Champions initiative, we started conducting high-level roundtable discussions, qualitative interviews, quantitative surveys, and workshop retreats with company leaders from small and medium-sized enterprises. Started in 2021, this project concluded its third year of collecting insights from SMEs and best practice case studies from different parts of the world. From 2021 to 2023, almost 1000 companies took part in the survey, where we quantitatively measured future readiness and its drivers as per the nomological network presented in the earlier chapter. After removing companies which identified themselves as large, we have a total of 835 companies in our global study, out of which 332 participated in 2021, 441 participated in 2022, and 62 participated in 2023.

Participants represented eight regions: (i) Asia Pacific, (ii) Eurasia, (iii) Europe, (iv) Latin America and Caribbean, (v) Middle East and North Africa, (vi) North America, (vii) South Asia, and (viii) Sub-Saharan Africa. There was also representation from 22 different industries as per the categorization of the International Labor Organization: agriculture, basic metal production, chemical industries, commerce, construction, education, financial services and professional services, food and beverage, forestry, health services, tourism and catering, mining, mechanical and electrical engineering, media, oil and gas production or oil refining, telecommunication services, public service, shipping and ports, textiles, transport (including civil aviation, railways, and road transport), transport equipment manufacturing, and utilities (water, gas, electricity). 62.2% of participants were from small companies (146 in 2021, 338 in 2022, 35 in 2023), 23.7% were medium-sized (101 in 2021,

77 in 2022, 20 in 2023), and 14.1% were mid-sized (85 in 2021, 26 in 2022, and 7 in 2023).

Participants of the quantitative study were asked to respond to items measuring the various variables presented in the nomological network on a scale from 1 (*strongly disagree*) to 5 (*strongly agree*). Items were adapted from established scales in literature. In this continuous project, we learnt from the data and insights from decision makers from all over the world, and made updates to the survey, measuring more relevant constructs as the project goes on.

Regional and Industry Differences

When I ran statistical analyses to determine regional and industry differences in innovation, financial performance, societal impact, and adaptive capacity, I surprisingly did not find significant differences. There were small differences in the levels of future readiness reported, but they were not statistically significant. There could be a few reasons for this, such as the following:

First, there were so many regions and industries represented that the sample size of companies per industry per region was not sufficient to induce an effect with statistical significance.

Second, executives were asked to respond to how their company was doing in relation to their peers or competitors. Companies in an industry that might be slow to change like, say, basic metal production, might still rate themselves similarly as a faster-moving industry like telecommunications, as they used their peers in the industry and their region as a benchmark and not all other companies.

Third, while the *amount* of innovation and societal impact may be similar across regions and industries, the *type* is different. For example, societal impact in the health industry could include innovations that provide more patients with easier access to health services, while in the agriculture industry, innovation and societal impact could include things like integrating AI in smart irrigation systems to minimize water waste and conserve the environment. Similarly, motivation for innovation in different regions differ, but may lead to similar results. In countries with governments that provide generous grants for small innovative companies, decision makers are incentivized to innovate. In countries

with less supportive governments, businesses can be pushed to innovate out of necessity. For example, "jugaad" is popularized in India as a flexible approach to problem-solving using limited resources in a creative way.

There are limitations to this study, but these are nonetheless encouraging results. What this could mean is that businesses can leverage the unique characteristics of their industry and find their niche problems to solve in a bid to improve their position in the chosen market while impacting the society and environment positively. In testing the nomological network described in the previous chapter, industry, region, and company size are controlled for.

Future Readiness

We looked at the three pillars of future readiness: long-term growth, societal impact, and adaptive capacity. In 2021, with the very recent impact of COVID-19 on businesses, it was presumed that the future readiness of SMEs would be low. We predicted lower-than-usual levels of innovation and financial performance, with goals related to societal impact taking a back seat. In 2022, in running the same survey, future readiness levels might increase or bounce back to pre-COVID levels. However, what we found was that the levels of long-term growth, societal impact, and adaptive capacity remained similar to those in 2021, suggesting that the impact of COVID-19 lasted longer even when lockdowns and travel restrictions were lifted (Figure 1).

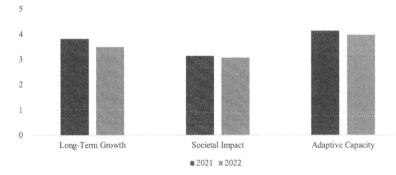

Figure 1. Future readiness data for 2021 and 2022.[a]

---

[a]2023 was not included due to the small sample size.

Another possible reason for these results is that while SMEs may be surviving better now as they found effective ways to manage the effects of the pandemic, new crises such as the ongoing war in Ukraine, the subsequent energy crisis, and hyperinflation, amid the continuously increasing demand for sustainable innovation, present new challenges for businesses to adapt to.

Long-Term Growth: Innovation

Despite the lack of resources, small-sized companies did not report having statistically significant lower levels of innovation than medium and mid-sized counterparts. In 2023, small companies in fact reported on average higher levels of innovation (3.47 out of 5) from the company than bigger companies (2.92 out of 5). We had a much smaller sample size in 2023, so this result must be interpreted with caution. However, it is still encouraging that we are seeing a trend where smaller companies are more empowered to innovate and disrupt the industries they are in.

Sustainability/Societal Impact

Where smaller companies consistently did worse than medium- and mid-sized companies over the years was in the societal impact dimension. Not only that, we also found that societal impact is consistently the lowest rated out of the three future dimension pillars. This is despite the enormous societal impact they can collectively have. This is corroborated by the finding that only 7% of all decision makers surveyed cited "sustainability" as a business challenge.

This is not to say that sustainability is "so easy" that it does not present itself as a challenge. It simply is not a top-of-mind issue for executives in SMEs. Understandably, executives' top challenges revolve around traditional business fundamentals, such as survival, expansion, access to funding, and talent. However, with the increasing demand from consumers for sustainability and from investors for ESG alignment, smaller companies can realize that increasing sustainability in their business decisions could lend them a competitive advantage.

Apart from factors related to survival, another possible reason why societal impact is not identified as a top challenge is that many SMEs may believe

themselves to be underprepared to engage in sustainable practices or believe themselves to be too small compared to larger organizations to have much impact. Many SMEs may also simply not consider including sustainability goals explicitly in their vision because they are already embedded within, or are organic by-products of, the organization's orientation and business model. For example, for several of the case study companies interviewed for this book, providing meaningful employment for potentially disadvantaged members of society is part of the company's business model to the extent that the challenges perceived by founders are related to the company's expansion or to the business model itself, as opposed to consciously pursuing sustainability goals. We explore in Chapter 4 on Sustainability how SMEs can leverage technology, among others, to pursue societal impact.

Adaptive Capacity

Smaller companies exhibited greater adaptive capacity. They were significantly more agile to make adaptations to their business strategies and offerings in response to the market. This was especially pronounced during the pandemic, when SMEs were able to engage in digital transformation processes faster without the obstacles presented by bureaucracy and the need for approval at multiple levels. Many also *needed* to adapt in order to survive. A study by *VISA* in August 2020 found that 67% of small businesses reported that they were pivoting: restaurants began selling make-at-home meal kits or opened general stores, fitness studios offered virtual classes, and family clinics offered telehealth consultations.[1]

However, small companies reported *lower* levels of organizational resilience. There were fewer slack resources to buffer the negative impacts, and the company's operations could not bounce back as easily as for larger companies. However, a common theme that was found in the founders whom I interviewed for this research pointed to the fact that organizational resilience does not come from the tangible resources a company has. Resilience comes from its *people*. We discuss this in several portions of the book, especially in Chapter 6 on Talent. Where SMEs lack in financial resources and manpower, they make up for with the tenacity of their employees in hard times.

Top Concerns

We asked all decision makers to list up to three things that "keep them up at night".[b] What are the main challenges that leaders of SMEs are occupied with?

Talent

In 2021, talent attraction and retention topped the challenges among SME decision makers with 52.5% of them citing it as one of the three main challenges they have in their business. In 2022, at 48%, this did not change much. Attracting the right kind of talent, and getting talent to stay in the company with the right skill set, proved to be difficult still. Compounded with the trend of the Great Resignation, where job candidates and employees value meaning and purpose, and are interested in working for companies that care for them, the traditional recipe to attract highly sought-after candidates is no longer successful. Instead of offering generous compensation packages and career progression opportunities, smaller companies now need to ensure that they provide employees less-tangible resources like welfare, mentorship, and ensuring that they act on employee feedback.

According to a 2022 survey by *Human Resources Online*, more employees are resigning now compared to 12 months ago. 49% of the managers surveyed said that "they are not finding it easy to deal with the Great Resignation", 65% found it difficult to hire or find replacements compared to a year ago, and 52% said they see few or no qualified applicants when they try to hire. In a *Qualtrics* survey in 2022, 58% of employees reported planning to shift careers in the same year, with a 13% decrease in levels of well-being compared to the year before.

One of the possible reasons is the lack of feeling cared for by the organization. 97% of the employees believed that it is important for their company to listen to feedback. While 74% admitted to having an opportunity to provide feedback, only 21% said that their company acts on feedback very well. With this in mind, it is important to ensure that HR frameworks are adapted accordingly to deal with this need from employees. Especially with the difficulty in finding

---

[b] Again, many of the statistics presented here are from 2021 and 2022 due to the small sample size in the study in 2023. However, there are references to qualitative data collected from our 2023 study.

qualified candidates, it is crucial for SMEs to be able to offer a satisfactory package — above and beyond monetary compensation — to increase the uptake rate of job offers. With the average training cost per employee to be highest among small businesses according to *Investopedia* statistics,[2] motivating these employees to stay in the organization is a top concern for SME business owners. This is especially so because funding and access to capital remained top challenges in 2022 and 2023.

Survival, Expansion, Funding & Access to Capital

Survival and expansion (43.8% in 2021 and 67% in 2022) and funding and access to capital (35.7% in 2021 and 24% in 2022) were the next challenges for SMEs after the concern for talent. One of the possible reasons for this is a less-than-favorable policy environment SMEs found themselves in, with 22% identifying it as a hindrance to reaching their goals.

For smaller companies, we found that *networks* were one way to gain access to financial resources. The more diverse the network that companies have, especially if they are able to mobilize these networks at short notice, the more future-ready are the companies. If SMEs align their business purpose to the objectives of investors and governments, often aimed toward sustainability, they can gain financial resources through investments and government grants. This is one way to counter the obstacle highlighted above in that institutions can have a supporting role for an environment conducive to SMEs in order to achieve their goals, including sustainability ones.

Drivers of Future Readiness
Business Orientation and Business Model

I ran a regression analysis testing the effects of the drivers of future readiness on the three pillars. Our hypotheses held true. Business orientation is positively related to future readiness. With more autonomy, proactiveness, innovativeness, (calculated) risk-taking, and competitive aggressiveness, SMEs are more future-ready. Indeed, making business decisions based on a culture conducive to innovation is positive for company outcomes. That is obvious. However, when I ran separate analyses based on company size, I found that business orientation was not a predictor for small companies. This means that the smaller the company, the less the internal workings of the organization help in increasing future readiness. Similar results were found for the relationships between business model and future readiness. Where then do small companies "derive" future readiness from?

Networks

The answer to the previous question lies in networks. Networks were very crucial for small companies. It is no secret that companies need help from their professional and personal networks when they are first starting out. However, one interesting finding is that networks play a huge role in getting small companies to engage in societal impact. When small companies are not embedded in important networks (e.g., a formal network system that brings many entrepreneurs from different industries together, ties to governmental agencies, etc.), they do not appear to be "motivated" to engage in societal impact.

This seeming lack of motivation does not mean that small companies do not wish to pursue sustainability, but rather, it could be that they lack the proper resources, such as informational resources, on *how* they could pursue sustainability. Networks to larger companies or mentors could help small companies kickstart their sustainability journey as they have access to knowledge on what it takes to create societal impact. Additionally, networks to governmental agencies could induce small companies to pursue objectives in line with a national sustainability agenda.

What we additionally observe is that the effect of networks diminishes with increasing size. Medium-sized and mid-sized companies rely *less* on networks to achieve higher levels of future readiness. This is an interesting transition as we observe that a small company starts out by seeking resources *external* to the organization, but as it grows and finds its path, increasingly examines resources *internal* to the organization and makes changes accordingly (to the business orientation or business model) to be more future-ready.

Digital Infrastructure

The results for digital infrastructure were mixed. After controlling for company size, industry, and region, digital infrastructure positively drives all three pillars of future readiness. When company size was not controlled for, digital

infrastructure is a significant predictor for long-term growth and adaptive capacity, but not societal impact. One possible reason is the increasing awareness of sustainability (albeit a low take-up rate among SMEs) and non-digital ways of pursuing it, such as increasing focus on inclusive hiring and reducing the company's carbon footprint non-digitally. While being updated with the latest technologies is important in today's economy, it might be useful to consider that digital technology is not necessarily the end goal. A clear vision, excellent leadership, and communication of shared beliefs might be a more sustainable approach in pursuing future readiness.

Governance

Governance was one aspect of the survey where respondents tended to find the most difficulty in answering, with a higher response rate of "Don't Know", compared to other questions. This means that decision makers in SMEs tend to be unclear on whether governance strategies or policies are part of their business operations — as they are not explicitly discussed or practiced. They might be an implicit part of management or a coincidental by-product of the company's process in value creation, but using governance as an explicit business strategy is generally new territory for SMEs. This supports our finding earlier that sustainability-related topics are not top-of-mind for a majority of SMEs as they focus on more pertinent issues, such as talent, expansion, and overcoming other barriers.

Governance is a significant driver for all three pillars of future readiness. Through a clearer vision wherein sustainability is embedded, and the appropriate execution of such a strategy, companies achieve higher levels of long-term growth, societal impact, and are also more agile in adapting to sustainability trends. Governance has an especially large effect on societal impact as expected.

An interesting finding is that *within* companies, they differ on the various dimensions of governance. Scores for governing purpose and strategy (having a written mission statement and stated purpose that includes an explicit commitment to sustainability) were highest, whereas scores for stakeholder engagement (including having formal procedures and designated teams to engage stakeholders) were lowest. A visual representation of the results of the five dimensions of governance is shown in Figure 2. Companies seem to be

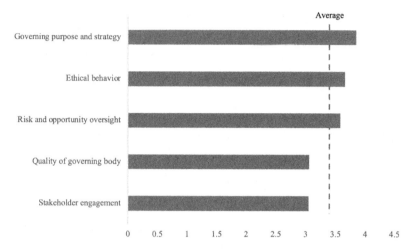

Figure 2. Scores on the five different dimensions of governance.

clear on a more conceptual level on what needs to be done, but are still some way from actually putting these concepts into practice.

Power of the People
Authentic Leadership

We discovered the role of authentic leadership in future readiness based on qualitative interviews and roundtable discussions with founders and top executives in our first wave of data collection in 2021. From 2022 onward, we empirically tested this by asking participants to respond to items measuring the four different aspects of authentic leadership. The results were convincing. There are large positive significant effects of authentic leadership on all three pillars of future readiness. Leadership in future-ready companies is less about the management of day-to-day business operations, but more about inspiring and engaging employees through higher values. Leaders who encourage seeking feedback, admitting and learning from mistakes, and living and breathing the organizational mission, better lead the path toward future readiness.

Talent Fit and Psychological Safety

Talent fit was also a predictor of all three pillars of future readiness. Talent fit was significantly more important in smaller companies. This emphasizes the

importance of finding the "right" people for the company and deeply understanding the profile of such a "right" person. For small companies, they appear to be more open to hiring candidates lower on technical qualifications, but with a higher cultural and value fit. This is driven by the belief that hard skills can be trained, but changing one's values is much more difficult.

Besides, with fewer resources, small companies need to prioritize roles that they hire based on technical qualifications and roles that can be learnt on the job. A more senior role like the chief operating officer or a senior software development engineer would require practical expertise and experience. Investing more resources into such senior roles means that there are fewer resources available to offer to junior positions. As we discuss in this book, in talent acquisition in small companies, a culture fit, together with a teachable attitude, becomes more important.

As predicted, psychological safety mediated the relationship between the Power of the People and future readiness, as these ingredients contribute to an environment where employees are empowered to bring the organization to greater heights.

Summary of Global Assessment

Integrating the findings presented above, as well as first-hand insights from leaders of future-ready SMEs, some of the noteworthy highlights are as follows:

1. **Sustainability** is recognized as an important factor for businesses to be future-ready. However, it is not top-of-mind for many decision makers in SMEs, with more immediate concerns proving to be more pertinent. It is crucial to maintain and grow businesses, attract and retain talent, and continue to have access to capital and funding. Companies that excel in sustainability and societal impact, however, tend to be those where ESG goals are already embedded in their vision and core business operations.

2. Our **global assessment** showed no significant differences in the future readiness of SMEs at the regional or industry level. Understandably, the *type* of societal impact companies can have in different regions and industries may differ. However, we found that the *level or amount* of societal impact remains relatively constant among different regions.

3. Strategy on paper is important, but the **execution of a company's mission and vision** is more predictive of the future readiness of the business. This requires leadership to communicate the vision to employees — a process that is easier in smaller companies due to flatter organizational structures — such that the vision is "lived and breathed" by members of the organization.

4. **Technology** is best used as a means to an end. While technology can accelerate innovative ideas and support an organization's mission, technology itself is not enough if the vision is not strong and clear. Nonetheless, it is important to keep up with technological infrastructure essential in the respective industries, including ensuring high levels of cybersecurity.

5. SMEs find strength in their **people**. Appealing to a higher purpose, smaller companies which attract and retain resourceful people who are aligned with the organizational mission find themselves to be in a better position to overcome crises, while saving on tangible resources like money. Again, strong leadership and an organizational culture that empowers employees give SMEs an edge in surviving difficult times as a cohesive unit.

6. **Networks** are especially important for small businesses when they are starting out for long-term growth, societal impact, and adaptive capacity, as they gain resources in the form of information, funding, and collaboration from their networks to further their business goals. As companies get bigger, they become less reliant on networks and use the information they learnt to make changes internally, i.e., to their orientation and business model in order to create value for society.

7. Future-ready SMEs tend to pursue **strategic growth**. They recognize that expansion may come at a cost to the organizational culture and their ability to be agile — and hence approach growth carefully to maintain the strengths they developed as a small company.

Now, let us explore in the following section the challenges SMEs face in the market environment and the practical recommendations from case study companies on how to overcome them.

Part Three

Challenges in the Market Environment

Chapter 4
Sustainability

Sustainability has been a buzzword in the business world for decades. The historical evolution of philanthropy and charity giving can be traced back to the early 20th century, and the rise of social and environmental movements in the 1950s and 1960s caused some businesses to pay more attention to the societal impact they were making. However, it is only recently that most businesses and consumers alike have placed an *actual* finger on what sustainability is. Environmental sustainability used to be understood as mainly comprising the 3 Rs of reduce, reuse, and recycle, when it covers exceedingly more. Sustainability goals were not easy to imagine, and many equated doing good for the society with engaging in philanthropy.

Now, sustainability has evolved into something much more than an abstract goal. In this chapter, I highlight the differences between the traditional approach of corporate social responsibility (CSR) and sustainability today, emphasize the importance of integrating sustainability in business strategies of all sizes, and feature case studies of companies pursuing sustainability in unique ways. Lastly, I will briefly cover impact investing in financing sustainability, as well as an important non-financial factor: networks.

CSR vs. ESG

Corporate social responsibility, or CSR, refers to business decisions which ensure that one's organization operates ethically. According to business ethics professors Archie Carroll and Ann Buchholtz, there are four layers of CSR, i.e., four ways businesses can fulfill their responsibilities to relevant stakeholders.[1] The first layer is economic responsibility, which is the company's responsibility to be profitable to ensure returns on investment to its shareholders and to pay its employees. The second layer is legal responsibility, where the company must operate within the regulatory framework. Companies should not engage in illicit activities. The third layer is ethical responsibility, which expands beyond compliance to rules and regulations and instead covers moral elements as expected by society. For instance, child labor is not necessarily illegal in some countries, but engaging in it arguably neglects a company's ethical responsibility. The fourth layer is philanthropic responsibility, which involves doing good deeds for other members of the public, making donations, and all in all being a good corporate citizen.

Today, much attention is focused on another three letters: ESG. ESG stands for Environmental, Social, and Governance. Compared to CSR, ESG represents a more quantitative measure of sustainability. It is a risk management approach that takes environmental, social, and governance considerations into account when designing and executing business strategies. CSR was also largely voluntary. Companies decided for themselves on what they wanted to do, which areas they wanted to focus on, and which key performance indicators (KPIs) they wanted to adhere to. While the CSR concept is not obsolete in today's business world, the lack of uniform measurement or global standard has resulted in various interpretations of what being a good corporate citizen exactly constitutes.

The repercussions of this can be seen in numerous cases of greenwashing, where companies invest more time and money in advertising that it is an environmentally friendly company than on *actually* minimizing harm to the environment. To adapt to increasing consumer demands for sustainability, several have taken the route of deceptively using marketing tactics to persuade stakeholders that their products and policies are sustainable, so that customers purchase their products and increase company profits. The carbon credit system,[a] initially devised to reduce greenhouse gas emissions, also saw negative consequences. Larger corporations could buy carbon credits from smaller companies to remain within their prescribed limit. Fossil fuel and airline

---

[a] Carbon credits, or carbon offsets, are part of a cap-and-trade program. Companies that pollute are awarded credits which allow them to continue to pollute up to a certain limit. Meanwhile, companies with unneeded credits may sell their credits to other companies which need them. Private companies are thus financially incentivized to reduce greenhouse emissions.[2]

companies, for example, could in turn legally use their credits to inform their customers that they are "carbon-neutral", without actively engaging in non-financial measures which mitigate their impact on the environment.

With the ESG approach, each of the three components is integrated in businesses' decision-making processes, from day-to-day operations to bigger strategic directions. For example, a company could commit to environmental sustainability by calculating and publishing its carbon footprint in measuring energy use efficiency, carbon emissions, and waste and water management. Commitment to social sustainability looks at a company's relationships with internal (e.g., employees) and external (e.g., customers) stakeholders and ensures that human rights, physical health, safety, and diversity, equity, and inclusion (DEI) are taken into consideration. Governance refers to the way companies use accurate and transparent accounting methods, are accountable to shareholders, and ensure ethical selection of leadership and board members and executives (e.g., avoiding conflicts of interest). In several instances, having executive compensation tied to the company's social and/or environmental performance is one way of ensuring the high quality of the firm's governing body.

On top of ESG, companies are also increasingly committing to one or several of the United Nations' 17 Sustainable Development Goals (UN SDGs). These UN SDGs and the UN Global Compact, which encourages businesses worldwide to adopt sustainable and socially responsible policies, have been around for quite some time (the UN Global Compact as early as 2000), but have never been binding. To remain future-ready, companies need to be proactive and use these guidelines not as lip service, but integrate them in their framework of making actionable business decisions.

B Corp Certification

There is an increasing number of companies which apply for a B Corp Certification. The B Corp Certification, handed out by B Lab Global, is a label afforded to businesses that meet high standards of verified performance, accountability, and transparency on various factors throughout a company's supply chain. Companies pursuing B Corp Certification must go through a highly rigorous review, providing information from employee benefits to input materials, and must make a legal commitment to their sustainability goals. B Corp Certification is costly, must be renewed every three years, and is only attached to that particular branch of the company. For instance, if a company has offices in Madrid, Jakarta, and Cartagena, and applied for B Corp Certification for the Madrid office, the branches in Jakarta and Cartagena must apply for B Corp separately. In September 2023, B Lab Global teamed up with Nasdaq OneReport to help companies streamline their processes and best showcase their ESG efforts. Despite the rigor and high costs involved, there is increasing enthusiasm from SMEs to apply for B Corp Certification. By getting sustainability "right" from the start, smaller companies do not have to overcome legacy business models to achieve B Corp status. Not only does this solidify a company's commitment to sustainability but attaining labels (much like ISO certifications) is also one way to attract positive attention from investors, customers, and other stakeholders.

Why SMEs Should Care about Sustainability

Much attention on sustainability has been placed on large multinational corporations — and rightly so. They have access to a wider pool of resources to create substantial change, and should indeed be held to higher standards for their environmental and social impact. However, as we look to the future and embrace new ways of remaining competitive, it is important for companies of all sizes to integrate sustainability into their business model.

Despite the buzz around sustainability, smaller companies struggle to have it on their business agenda. In a survey of 773 small and medium-sized companies across the globe, only 7% of decision-makers cited sustainability as a top challenge they faced.[3] Understandably, executives' top challenges revolve around some of the traditional business fundamentals such as survival, expansion, access to funding, and talent acquisition and retention. Sustainability can also be an added risk for SMEs, as more resources need to be poured into these initiatives, and time and energy spent on sustainability strategies may take away resources from core products and services in an already lean operating business model.

However, this is in stark contrast to broader societal expectations. The 2022 Edelman Trust Barometer reported that 59% of respondents believed that businesses were not doing enough for climate change and 49% said that businesses were not doing enough for economic inequality. Further, 58% of them would buy from or advocate for brands based on their beliefs and values, 60% would choose a place to work based on their beliefs and values, and 88% of institutional investors would subject ESG aspects to the same scrutiny as operational and financial considerations.[4] SMEs *need* to keep up with the increasing demands surrounding sustainability from multiple stakeholders in order to be future-ready.

Again, it is important to emphasize here that sustainability is not only about environmental conservation (E) but also about furthering human well-being (S) and responsible stakeholder management (G). ESG is one way for companies to design, implement, and measure the impact of sustainability initiatives. In a volatile, uncertain, complex, and ambiguous (VUCA) world, sustainability can be perceived as one of the strategies that lend companies a competitive advantage. However, when the global pandemic hit, and when we found ourselves at the apex of a VUCA situation, we learnt that sustainability not only lent companies a competitive advantage; it became a *necessity*.

As an example, digitalization as a sustainable strategy found its way to the forefront. Companies delivering physical products needed to digitize themselves — the physical presence of stores or offices was no longer sufficient. Customers needed to be able to find products online, and brands needed a digital presence to continue to survive. Inadvertently, this fulfilled SDG 9 of building resilient infrastructure and sustainable industrialization. Digitalization in poorer countries also encouraged universal access to information and communications technology (SDG 9) and working remotely from these regions allowed workers to access jobs through technology (SDG 8: Decent Work).

Clients and suppliers were pushed to think of new ways to deliver products and services in an effective yet sustainable way. Ideas that received pushback prior to the pandemic became the new modus operandi. For example, the idea of using video interviews for hiring has been around for some time, as recruitment companies have leveraged technology to revolutionize the hiring process and have suggested that their client companies use video interviews as a form of assessment of their candidates. This idea used to be rejected by recruiters who believed that video interviews lacked aspects of the body language which may provide better cues on the suitability of candidates. However, at the onset of the COVID-19 pandemic, digital delivery of services through video interviews became the norm as in-person interviews were not allowed due to physical restrictions, and masks could also hide facial expressions.

In the comfort of one's own home, without facial masks, candidates could now save time, money, and their carbon footprint from commuting, while opening up their schedule to attend more interviews. When video interviews were asynchronous, that is, they were recorded previously and recruiters could look at these videos at a later time, recruiters also saved time when they could make decisions regarding a candidate within the first few minutes of the interview and saved money on reimbursing transport costs to candidates. This example showed how a tumultuous event could significantly change the perception of the viability of a sustainable strategy. Where it was previously met with resistance, the same strategy could now be the new style of working.

This type of shift in mindset is especially important in future readiness of SMEs. Recognizing that smaller companies have many immediate problems (also known as "mini-crises") to solve, many stakeholders to answer to, and are in constant firefighting mode, sustainability may not be their top priority. However, if SMEs recognize that *integrating* sustainability in their business model, rather than considering it *after* the economic responsibility is fulfilled, is beneficial, they can make vastly different decisions and optimize their resources to pursue financial and sustainability goals simultaneously.

Featured Case Study Companies: E, S, and G

Despite the enormous societal impact that SMEs collectively have as described earlier in this book, smaller companies rank lower on societal impact compared to other dimensions of future readiness. In Chapter 5, I outline how smaller companies can leverage technology to create positive societal impact and use their competitive advantages to make a pivot to sustainability. In this chapter, I feature three case study companies that pursue sustainability through creativity, resilience, passion, and a guiding framework. The three companies also come from very different industries and range in size, highlighting the different possible ways in which SMEs can embody ESG and contribute to the global sustainability agenda.

Sustainability in Art and Fashion: Environmental

rehyphen®, Singapore

From a humble exhibition in Shanghai, China, to having customers approaching the company for customized orders, rehyphen® has come a long way in redefining sustainability in art and fashion. rehyphen® is an initiative set up by Jessica J.J. Chuan, who studied fashion in New York, which involves collecting discarded cassette tapes and turning this e-waste into art. Through a special weaving technique, these tapes are turned into a piece of MusicCloth®, which is then used in fashion accessories, stationery, and lifestyle items like the MusicCloth® clutch bag, MusicCloth® notebook, and MusicCloth® city map poster. Examples of these products are provided in the Appendix.

At a time where music and audio recordings are digitized and cassette tapes are no longer widely used, rehyphen® reduces the negative impact of this type of waste on the environment while giving the product new life, tackling the "Environmental" aspect of ESG. Chuan shared how her resilience got rehyphen® to where it is today: "Back then, sustainability was not a big thing in China. People did not know much about sustainability, recycling, and this kind of concept. Our first exhibition was not really well-received. But it's okay, it's like an education process for the customer."

Chuan further shares, "From there, we received quite a lot of media (and) press (attention). And then, it's like a snowballing effect. Some retailers approached us, and we participated with a fair, kind of a big fair, to get (a wider) audience. And slowly, we have our first online store." Indeed, after two years, rehyphen® has now collected "too many tapes". Being quick on their feet, rehyphen® thought of new ways of recycling the increasing amount of discarded cassette tapes. They created "Tweet Tape", where customers could type in 140 characters on the end of a tape, to be used as a greeting card.

"When they give [the greeting card] to someone they love, they are actually passing (on) the sustainability message at the same time. So when people receive this gift, they can turn it and read the message inside." Spreading awareness about sustainability and saving the environment are integral to rehyphen®'s philosophy. This small Singapore-based enterprise regularly launches workshops to educate the public, such as through collaborations with the Ministry of Environment and Water Resources (now called Ministry of Sustainability and the Environment) and the Development Bank of Singapore. It also offers these workshops to visitors from overseas as unique experiences.

rehyphen®, however, does not forget the business value of its products. Recognizing that there will be fewer and fewer cassette tapes available, it is able to price its products at a premium. "We started [selling our products] at S$20. But five years later, we can price them at S$98 because the resources become less and less," mentioned Chuan.

Lastly, rehyphen® emphasizes the nostalgia associated with cassette tapes. Sometimes, customers approach Chuan to recycle their tapes into collectible items. For instance, one customer's audio recording of the interviews she did for her doctoral dissertation over 20 years ago was turned into pieces of art, which were then gifted to the customer's advisor and an interview participant. After converting the tapes to fashion pieces or art, rehyphen® provides QR codes for customers to scan and listen to their customized playlists — holding on to the music aspect of these tapes.

The case study of rehyphen® shows us that sustainability does not have to be restricted to industrial or tech companies, but can be integrated in a way that enhances our personal lives through art. Today, rehyphen® boasts collaborations with prestigious companies like Singapore Airlines, through the bold choices of a fashion designer who wanted to make the world a better place.

Appendix

Sample Products Made from rehyphen®'s MusicCloth®

Source: rehyphen® Brand Book, 2023.[5]

Sustainability in Hospitality: Social

Salinda Resort, Phú Quốc, Vietnam

Salinda Resort is an award-winning luxury boutique located in Phú Quốc, an island east of mainland Vietnam. A famous tourist destination both among locals and foreigners, Phú Quốc boasts unspoiled beaches, spacious green parks, forests, sacred temples and pagodas, traditional villages, and connections to remote islands. The island has a population of about 180,000 out of Vietnam's 99 million residents.

Owned and developed by a Vietnamese family, Salinda opened in 2014. According to CEO Sandra Nguyen Si, opening a hotel or resort was initially not on the horizon for the family. However, when they visited Phú Quốc island about 15 years ago, they "fell in love with the whole greenness" of the island. At that time, there were few roads, no international airport, and the only way to access the island was by ferry. As they were toying with the idea of building a home on the island to retire to, they decided that it will be "boring" to live alone and needed some neighbors on this pristine island. "So we thought, let's open a hotel and we will have many neighbors. This is how it all started: an idea of having just a beach house in Phú Quốc turned into a 121-room beach house for everybody," said Nguyen Si.

Environmental sustainability is a huge part of Salinda's design and daily operations. 70% of the resort's land is dedicated to greenery with over 100 types of trees and flowers. The most sustainable wood in the world, Accoya,[b] is used in the architecture of the resort, technology is leveraged to ensure eco-friendly electricity usage and sewage purification treatment, and glass, ceramic, and kraft paper are used to replace plastic throughout the resort. Even though Salinda has won various awards and accolades (a list of Salinda's awards is provided in the Appendix) for its strides in sustainability and hospitality, one thing that stands out is its commitment to the "Social" aspect of ESG.

Salinda's vision, also known as "The Purple Purpose", highlights the role of giving back to the local Phú Quốc community.[6] Often referred to as "our

---

[b] Production of Accoya wood uses renewable resources and requires little energy, thus reducing greenhouse gas emissions. The wood itself absorbs carbon dioxide from the atmosphere, reducing its carbon footprint and remaining CO_2 negative during its full life cycle.

brothers and sisters", employees of Salinda are pivotal in carrying out Salinda's vision of "helping our community, cherishing our culture, and promoting diversity on Phú Quốc". On the company website, it states, "In Salinda, we believe that the community we live in is measured by the compassionate actions of its members." Beyond the company website, this vision is lived and breathed on the ground.

Many of the staff employed were born and raised in Phú Quốc. Salinda provides staff housing on the resort property, where the "brothers and sisters" eat, live, work, and go out together. Nguyen Si further elaborated, "They are becoming like this sort of family. It is not like 'Oh I see you in the morning, goodbye.' You can feel that all the time they care about each other and learn about each other. I think that created such a close connection or relationship work-wise."

Indeed, the close relationships among staff members result in excellent hospitality. When resort employees are able to rely on each other for help, guests benefit from superior customer service as problems get resolved quickly. For example, if an employee experiences language barriers with a guest, his or her colleague (or rather, "brother" or "sister") quickly assists to help understand and attend to the guest's query.

Salinda further places the local community at the forefront through civic activities such as scheduled neighborhood cleanups, cooking for the homeless, and hosting underprivileged children. Vietnamese culture is also integrated and displayed in Salinda's daily operations. Handmade ceramicware from the Bát Tràng village is used for breakfast tea or coffee, paintings by Vietnamese artists are displayed (and are for sale) in rooms and public areas, and the gift shop features locally made handicrafts in collaboration with a non-profit organization that creates sustainable employment for underprivileged women. As Salinda contributes to booming tourism to Phú Quốc, this inadvertently leads to improvement in local infrastructure such as more roads and the building of a new airport.

With 235 employees, including a diverse team with people from Southeast Asia, Salinda is able to make a positive social impact despite its small size. The resort excels in serving its stakeholders of guests, employees, as well as the local community. One is then brought back to the owners' original intent for

Salinda: a beach house for everybody, where guests feel like neighbors and employees feel like family. Committed to creating a "home-from-home" feeling, leaders and employees at Salinda prioritize genuine, authentic, and meaningful relationships. This is probably why Salinda ranks so highly among guests since it opened, even though sustainable tourism gained significant popularity only recently.[c]

Sandra Nguyen Si sums this up nicely. When asked which factor was most important in leading a future-ready company — finances, talent, leadership, networks, or market environment — Nguyen Si answered, "Heart".

Appendix

List of Salinda's Awards

---

[c] Global tourism steadily increased up until 2020, where much importance was placed on leisure travel and business travel. According to the UN Intergovernmental Panel on Climate Change, as of 2022, 81% of travelers worldwide believe that sustainable travel is important.

Sustainability in Construction: Governance

City Developments Ltd., Singapore

"Nearly 29 years ago when I mentioned green building or sustainability, people thought I was crazy. Now, they ask me for tips on how to integrate sustainability into the business, and how we have managed to create a business case for sustainability." Esther An, Chief Sustainability Officer, started the sustainability journey of Singapore's global real estate company City Developments Limited (CDL) back in 1995. Recognizing that the construction sector makes up 40% of global greenhouse gas (GHG) emissions, An knew that the building and construction industry could do more to contribute to the environment and society positively.

CDL is a leading real estate company with a network spanning 143 locations in 28 countries and regions.[d] However, when An started her role in CDL, not only was it a much smaller company but sustainability was also not on the business agenda. "At most, we talked about environmental conservation and CSR," said An. Without an established sustainability strategy like most companies then, An drew inspiration from the triple bottom line principle of People, Planet, and Profit established by John Elkington.

CDL understood the need to maintain profitable as a business and in returning value to its investors and shareholders. To include the "people" and "planet" aspects in the triple bottom line, An thought the best way to communicate this to others was through using simple language. Thus, the corporate ethos was created: "Conserving as we Construct". CDL takes into consideration both the social and environmental impact of its operations as it is in the business of building spaces for people and communities and aims to do so while minimizing its carbon footprint. An reflected, "These four words seem so simple, but if you think deeper, it is relevant in everything we do, and even more relevant today as the world is faced with a climate emergency."

As part of CDL's commitment to sustainability, it was the first Singapore company to publish its first sustainability report in 2008. Since 2015, this has developed into an Integrated Sustainability Report (ISR), which creates and captures value by using the six International Integrated Reporting Council (IIRC) capitals — financial, manufactured, organizational, social, human, and

---

[d] Information accurate as of 31 December 2022.

natural capital. Through its report, CDL shows how it fulfills its responsibilities to major stakeholders while also providing evidence of business value. CDL has formal processes to integrate economic, environmental, and social issues in the business strategy of the company, it has a formal stakeholder engagement plan that identifies relevant stakeholder groups, and its stated purpose includes creating value for all stakeholders, including shareholders. A sample page of the ISR is provided in the Appendix.

CDL sets high standards for its suppliers in complying with the reporting for Scope 1, Scope 2, and Scope 3 emissions.[e] As part of its efforts to measure and manage its emissions, CDL was the first real estate company in Singapore to set Science Based Targets Initiative (SBTi)-validated GHG reduction targets based on the 2°C warmer scenario in 2018. In December 2021, CDL renewed its SBTi-validated GHG emissions reduction targets to align with a 1.5°C warmer scenario. CDL is also the only Singapore company to be recognized in the 2022 CDP A List and the only company in Southeast Asia and Hong Kong to be listed on the CDP A List for five consecutive years.[f] CDL stresses the importance of staying ahead of the competition as it "not only helps the business, but also saves the planet".

This action-oriented strategy from CDL displays its high level of future readiness. In Singapore, the carbon tax was set at S$5 (around US$3.66) per tonne of GHG emissions ("/tC0$_2$e") from 2019 to 2023. This will progressively increase to S$25/tC0$_2$e (around US$18.30) in 2024, S$45/tC0$_2$e (around US$32.95) in 2026, and S$80/tC0$_2$e (around US$58.55) in 2030.[8] With carbon tax rates increasing to 9 times the current rate within less than five years, companies need to act quickly to secure their competitiveness in the future market environment. As mentioned previously, CDL goes above and beyond mere compliance to regulations. Instead, it actively engages its internal and external stakeholders and makes changes to not only adapt to but also *create* a better future.

---

[e] Scope 1 emissions refer to direct emissions from sources which are owned and controlled by a company, including emissions from transport (combustion of fuel), manufacturing, or production of electricity (burning coal). Scope 2 emissions refer to emissions released into the atmosphere from the use of purchased energy. Scope 3 emissions include all other indirect emissions that occur across the value chain and outside of the organization's direct control, such as emissions from extraction and production of purchased materials, transportation of purchased fuels, and employees' commute.[7]
[f] CDP is one of the founding partners of the SBTi and plays a pivotal role in accelerating and institutionalizing science-based target-setting as global best practice. To be on the CDP A List, companies must receive an "A" score in aspects like climate change and water security.

Although CDL has become a large enterprise now, this future-ready mindset had been present in its earlier days. In 2005, back when the Green Mark — a certification scheme that evaluates a building's environmental impact — was introduced in Singapore, companies could apply for certification on a voluntary basis. An knew that it was simply a matter of time before this voluntary certification would become required by law. As such, CDL hopped onto this train early and invested in green building technology, innovations, and asset enhancement initiatives. Indeed, from 2008 onward, those who wish to develop a plot of land must adhere to the Green Mark certification. To date, CDL has amassed 120 Green Mark Awards, which included Green Mark Platinum, Green Mark Gold Plus, Green Mark Gold, and Green Mark Pearl.[9,10] A non-exhaustive list of CDL's awards and accolades is provided in the Appendix.

Fulfilling the "Governance" aspect of ESG is possible for smaller companies. When asked what SMEs can do with limited resources to invest in technologies for sustainability, An advised, "Smaller companies should start looking at doing a smaller scale audit of their business operations. It's a simple thing one can do, like a medical check. From a medical check, you can find out where your health problem lies. Similarly, companies can conduct a materiality study to assess their current ESG state and gaps. It does not have to be huge, but they can start asking simple questions like 'What does sustainability mean to your internal stakeholders?', 'Who are your key external stakeholders?' and this can be the suppliers, the media, banks, and your investors."

Above and beyond overseeing sustainability in CDL as part of her role, An is an advocate for sustainability through her speaking engagements around the globe, and sits on the boards or advisory platforms of international organizations including the Global Reporting Initiative (GRI), the Global Real Estate Sustainability Benchmark (GRESB) Foundation Board, and the UN Principles for Responsible Investment (PRI) Real Estate Advisory Committee. She also chairs the Singapore Sustainability Reporting Advisory Committee, the World Green Building Council Corporate Advisory Board, and the Asia Pacific Real Estate Association's ESG Committee. In addition, she founded the Women4Green and Youth4Climate networks in CDL to empower women and youths to champion climate action and sustainable development.

Appendix

Sample Page from CDL's Integrated Sustainability Report 2023

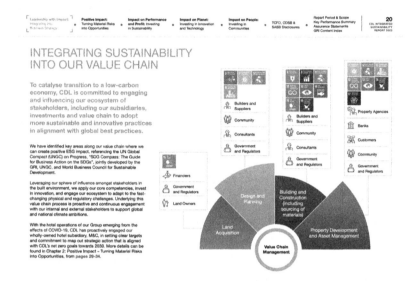

Non-Exhaustive List of CDL's Awards and Accolades for Sustainability

7ᵗʰ Asia Sustainability Reporting Awards	HR Asia Awards 2022	Singapore Business Review Technology Excellence Awards
• Asia's Report of the Year • Asia's Best Sustainability Report (Large Company) – Gold • Asia's Best Sustainability Reporting (CEO Letter) – Gold • Asia's Best Materiality Reporting – Gold • Asia's Best Climate Reporting – Gold • Asia's Best Sustainability Report (Governance) – Bronze	• Best Companies to Work for in Asia **HR Fest Awards 2022 (organised by HRM Asia)** • Employer of Choice **Royal Society for the Prevention of Accidents (RoSPA) Awards 2022**	• "Technology Excellence Award for Mobile - Real Estate" for CityNexus app **Singapore Governance and Transparency Index 2022** • Ranked joint 4ᵗʰ out of 489 companies
Climate Reporting in ASEAN – State of Corporate Practices 2022 • Top-ranked Singapore company	• Order of Distinction (for 17 consecutive Golds) **SGBC-BCA Leadership in Sustainability Awards 2022**	**Singapore HEALTH Award 2022** • Organisational Champion (Excellence)
Environmental Finance Sustainable Company Awards 2022 • Net Zero Progression of the Year, APAC	• Community Engagement Award - Singapore Sustainability Academy (SSA) • Urban Renewal Award - South Beach	**Steward Leadership 25 (2022)** • One of 25 companies in APAC region listed for steward leadership action
FT-Nikkei-Statista Climate Leaders Asia Pacific 2022 • Only Singapore property company recognised		

This list is not exhaustive. For a full listing of CDL corporate and project awards, please refer to www.cdl.com.sg. For a full listing of CDL sustainability awards, please refer to www.cdlsustainability.com.

Sustainability and Vision

These case study companies show how important stakeholders can start sustainability initiatives to tackle the Environmental, Social, or Governance aspects of ESG. rehyphen®, Salinda, and CDL have one thing in common: vision. This vision could either be created at the start or stumbled upon. When the vision is clear, and when leadership is passionate about this vision, we see how sustainability can be integrated into the business model so much so that sustainability *creates* value and does not take away from it. The importance of vision, and what constitutes good vision, is further expounded upon in Chapter 5. To close off this chapter, we explore the different ways of financing sustainability and the importance of networks in learning about sustainability.

Financing Sustainability

Impact Investing

Impact investing refers to the act of making investments with the intention of generating positive, measurable environmental and social impact along with financial returns. Even though there are moral reasons to support sustainability-oriented enterprises, investors must maintain a fiduciary responsibility and invest at the appropriate risk level.[11] As such, impact investing involves balancing financial viability, monetary return expectations, and social impact.

We observe impact investments primarily in social enterprises, which refer to companies that are for-profit, but have created a good or service that provides significant social impact. In smaller enterprises or emerging companies, microfinancing is also increasingly popular, which involves lending small amounts of money to individuals or groups of individuals who then use the money to fund their own businesses. These individuals or groups could belong to vulnerable segments of the population, such as women or the poor.

The International Finance Corporation (IFC), a member of the World Bank Group, is one of the oldest, largest, and best-known impact investors. It invests in a large range of projects, from private equity investments to large-scale infrastructure projects. Using what we call a Social Impact Map, investors assess the mission, social goals, inputs, activities, outputs, outcomes, and impact of organizations.[12] In addition to assessing the quality of these components (e.g., What social or environmental challenge is the organization addressing? What kind of human resources, capital, and materials is the organization investing in to achieve its goals? What output indicators will capture the essence of the impact? How well-organized is the company's management and board to deliver on the objectives?), impact investors also assess how far along the organization is on the Social Impact Map.

Smaller companies are understandably riskier than larger companies. The management is not as developed, there is lack of excess cash, and "high-risk" approvals often mean that equity holders demand higher compensation for the risk. It is therefore crucial for SMEs to closely align with sustainability goals set by investors. One way smaller companies can achieve this is by crafting a robust Social Impact Map, with measurable outputs and outcomes to present a business case to impact investors.

Alternative Ways of Funding Sustainability

It is not easy for SMEs to borrow from banks. Banks hesitate to approve loans to entities with lack of collateral, and similar to the abovementioned case with investors, "high-risk" approvals are hit with high interest rates for repayment — an additional hurdle for SMEs who already possess very few resources. When SMEs turn to international loans, international lenders face currency risk, which refers to a situation where they are left with losses if the local currency depreciates. This translates into risks often being pushed back to the borrowers, and founders of SMEs often find themselves in a resource loss spiral.

However, there are several other ways to fund sustainability. Government grants that support and encourage sustainability in businesses represent one such outlet. Smaller companies can position their business activities in a way that fulfills the criteria for available funding opportunities. For example, under the European Green Deal, the EU has various funding programs, such as Horizon Europe, LIFE, and the Innovation Fund, for companies pursuing eco-innovation and the EU Ecolabel. Other examples include Bethnal Green Ventures in London, which support founders using technology to tackle social problems and using "tech for good", VertueLab, which provides grants for cleantech start-ups, and 100+ Accelerator in Toronto, which collaborates with companies to achieve their 2025 Sustainability Goals.[13] When executives of start-ups and small companies align with broader social and economic development goals set by investors and the government, this can unlock new opportunities offered by start-up accelerators, incubators, and venture capitalists. Here, sustainability should be integrated into the business model and not treated like a side project.

Learning about Sustainability: Importance of Networks

Achieving societal impact or adopting sustainable business strategies is typically outside of small companies' immediate goals. Despite advocating for sustainability, sometimes smaller companies simply do not have access to the right tools. For instance, if they receive very little guidance on what a proper Social Impact Map looks like, they might still lose out on valuable investment. Grants are also not sustainable streams of capital. They could end abruptly, depending on government election cycles, and global events such as the pandemic could shift the country's priorities on how the government utilizes financial reserves.

This is where networks are important. Personal and professional networks can provide SMEs with financial and non-financial resources through information-sharing, partnerships, and affiliations with influential bodies. Valuable information on *how* to manage risks associated with sustainability and ways of measuring societal impact could be received from these networks. When small companies are connected to networks which can provide insights on future readiness and advice on how to keep up with the competition, they can learn from their networks or mentors about strategies on how to integrate sustainability effectively into their business agenda.

This assertion is research-backed. Our analysis from the WEF study found that although smaller companies ranked lower on societal impact, those with affiliation to important networks reported higher engagement in sustainability initiatives. There seems to be a positive effect for sustainability simply by maintaining and engaging in important relationships. This could be due to founders receiving valuable information and financing from their networks with regard to sustainability, as well as an overall push toward this agenda as their larger network recognizes the value of ESG in becoming future-ready.

Chapter 5
Technology

In today's ever-evolving digital landscape, technological advancements are reshaping the way businesses operate at an unprecedented pace. Small and medium-sized enterprises (SMEs) stand at the crossroads of innovation, facing unique challenges and opportunities compared to their larger multinational counterparts. While both SMEs and large corporations are compelled to adapt to emerging technological trends, SMEs must often navigate resource constraints and scalability issues with a different lens. As they embrace the digital era, SMEs should pay close attention to trends that can level the playing field, such as cloud computing, automation, and artificial intelligence. In this era of transformation, even tools like ChatGPT, which leverage the power of natural language processing, are becoming accessible and indispensable for SMEs. This chapter explores the technological trends reshaping SMEs' landscapes and delves into how these enterprises can harness the potential of innovations like ChatGPT to drive growth, improve customer experiences, and stay competitive in an increasingly tech-driven world.

The previous paragraph was completely written by ChatGPT. While that paragraph somewhat encapsulates the gist of this chapter, it required several prompts from me to be more specific about the current technological trends. The points made by ChatGPT were also rather general and did not tell us something we do not already know. It made my writing easier, but without multiple prompts and more detailed input, the output was "so-so". It would have been of higher quality with more concrete examples, which would have required a further prompt from me.

This is one example that shows the usability of AI. It saved considerable time in producing an initial product, but required multiple, more precise, instructions to produce a modified output of incremental quality. The quality of the output is acceptable based on the pooled data from other sample paragraphs on the platform, but if I wanted something of higher quality, significant human intervention will be needed. Just like in businesses, the quality of the output is highly dependent on the quality of input data, and SMEs need to get that right in their first steps of digitalization and leveraging AI.

In this chapter, among others, I will explore the potential of technologies like artificial intelligence for SMEs, including the risks involved. SMEs can indeed leverage technology to achieve higher levels of future readiness, and here we pay more special attention to using technology to create societal impact. First, this chapter describes dilemmas faced by SME executives with regard to technology. Then, we take a closer look at how digital infrastructure in a company impacts organizational goals. Spoiler alert: It is important, but not the most important aspect.

"Technological Noise"

Decisions around technology and digital innovation often plague decision makers of small and medium-sized enterprises. There are several reasons for this. First, changes in technology are so rapid in today's market environment that SMEs are often playing "catch-up" to ensure that their products and services are not obsolete in view of the current technological trends. Larger firms stay ahead of the curve as they have more resources invested into research and development of technological products and services, and are also capable of acquiring start-ups and infuse their innovative services as part of the big company's offering. SMEs, on the other hand, cannot simply "buy" these digital innovations. They would have to find other ways to gain access to digital solutions.

Second, the sheer number of digital and technological trends makes this overwhelming for most decision makers. According to Stanislas Bocquet, the founder and CEO of PALO IT, a mid-sized digital services company with 18 offices across Europe, Asia Pacific, and the Americas, "The world is accelerating exponentially. When I started this company in 2009, there were five technology trends. Now, we have perhaps 50 technology trends." Indeed, with many proposed digital solutions available to solve a myriad of problems, decision makers find it difficult to create an efficient digital strategy amid the "technological noise".

Third, despite the opportunities presented by some technological trends, they carry high levels of risk and uncertainty. Top executives of smaller companies need to make strategic decisions on which particular technologies to invest in. The massive tech layoff in 2022 — there were reportedly more than 100,000 layoffs from mature tech companies like Twitter, Microsoft, Lyft, and Snapchat, as well as from a few start-ups — heightened SMEs' hesitance to explore newer technologies. For example, despite the attempt at popularizing the concept of a metaverse for smaller businesses to virtualize their shops and reach more customers, the huge layoffs at Facebook — 11,000 people were laid off in November 2022 from metaverse projects — spread uncertainty, especially to smaller companies, which are less able to afford to make mistakes in decisions related to risky business initiatives. At the time of writing, there were a reported 164,744 layoffs in 2022 in 1,060 tech companies. In 2023,[1] this number rose to over 260,000 employees.[a]

Perceived Importance vs. Ability for Digital Innovation

Top executives of SMEs recognize that technology and digital innovation are important facets of the business. 25% of those who responded in the 2022 global study on Future Readiness of SMEs and mid-sized companies identified technology as one of their top challenges. In particular, they cited factors such as "having products and innovation that keep up with current technological demands from the market", "developing and implementing technological processes, e.g., automation", and experiencing difficulties in starting and implementing digital transformation in the company. According to OECD, smaller companies tend to lag on technology adoption and digitalization compared to their larger peers.[2] This statistic was further confirmed by the global study with 773 SMEs and mid-sized companies that I conducted with the World Economic Forum in 2021 and 2022. When assessing the level of digital infrastructure a company has, smaller firms reported lower levels compared to bigger firms.

As highlighted earlier in the nomological network of future readiness, digital infrastructure refers to an IT portfolio that a company has and includes technologies such as cloud computing, social media, and business analytics. When responding to items assessing digital infrastructure, smaller companies

---

[a] For the latest figures on tech layoffs, visit www.layoffs.fyi.

indicated that their employees do have access to a range of new technologies such as cloud, mobile, and big data analytics. However, where small companies tended to lack most was in being able to allocate adequate financial resources and/or talent needed to innovate within the company's IT portfolio. It is important to note that investments in technology and digital transformation do not only include the costs of these technologies themselves, but also in training employees to be well-versed in technologies that are yet to be mature, in roles that are yet to exist.

Data Readiness

According to a study in 2023 with 42 countries and 21 industries, many SMEs have yet to appoint specific roles to design and implement data strategies. 63% reported not having a Chief Privacy Officer (CPO), 60% did not have a Chief Data Officer (CDO), and 60% lacked a Chief Information Security Officer (CISO).[3] The lack of dedicated personnel for data management could be due to several reasons. First, budget constraints mean that SMEs are motivated to save on headcount. Second, employees of SMEs typically fulfill multiple roles as functions are coordinated laterally as opposed to vertically. While there may not be enough workload for a full-time data officer role, current employees may subsume data-related tasks in their current role. Third, the creation of this role may not yet be required by local regulations, and SMEs prioritize while they optimize.

Not only do lower levels of digital infrastructure mean that smaller companies are lagging behind when it comes to being able to innovate digital products and services to better serve the evolving market, but given that some experts highlight the role of technology in being pivotal in pursuing the global sustainability agenda, SMEs also miss out on creating value that has positive environmental and social impact. Executives of SMEs are cognizant of the importance of digital innovation, but struggle to execute within their constraints. With increased accessibility to technology and AI (as the ChatGPT introduction of this chapter rightly mentioned), we hope to highlight to smaller companies that they can indeed be in a better position to realize technological solutions for future readiness.

Artificial Intelligence (AI) and Digitalization: Benefits and Risks

Benefits of AI

There are various categorizations with regard to AI. Data ScienceTech Institute breaks down AI to three pillars: symbols, neurons, and graphs.[4] CaseGuard puts forward that artificial intelligence includes the five basic components of learning, reasoning, problem-solving, perception, and language understanding.[5] There are further layers added to AI with principles of AI research and ethical AI, relating to transparency, reproducibility, and responsibility. Essentially, artificial intelligence refers to learning mechanisms done by machines. There is some debate on whether decisions derived from AI are mimicking those arrived at by human intelligence, or whether they should mimic human decisions at all. At its core, artificial intelligence refers to the ability of a machine to learn decision patterns based on data inputs, algorithms, and deep learning (learning by example).

As consumers, we experience AI in our daily lives when we see travel and shopping recommendations based on our browsing data, when interacting with customer service chatbots, and when using apps to regulate our physical health, such as using sleep data to improve quality of sleep and predicting the optimal time to wake up. AI is entering the business world not only when it comes to offering products and services but also when it comes to improving internal business processes.

At a time where companies have access to more data than ever before, AI is no longer a novel technology used by a select few, but rather is integral in the future of work. According to *Forbes*, the amount of data created, captured, copied, and consumed in the world grew by almost 5,000% between 2010 and 2020.[6] Companies realize that data captured from customers and across their value chain can be used to make informed business decisions.

There is incentive to be early adopters of AI. According to Grand View Research, the global AI market size was valued at $136.55 billion in 2022, and is projected to expand at a compound annual growth rate of 37.3% from 2023 to 2030.[7] It is no surprise that large companies like Microsoft, Google, and Amazon are industry leaders in AI. But, where are the opportunities for SMEs?

Automation for Speedier Processes and More Consistent Service

Automation boosts process efficiency and can improve the speed or consistency of service. Process automation refers to the use of digital technology to handle processes and streamline them. This typically involves a combination of interactive software, bots, and machine learning. Digital Process Automation (DPA) refers to a type of automation which uses software to streamline or automate end-to-end workflows, tasks, and activities. In this way, DPA removes as much manual work involved in routine and repetitive tasks and processes as possible. Robotic Process Automation (RPA) is a software technology that makes it easy to build, deploy, and manage software robots that emulate human actions interacting with digital systems and software. Here, software robots — instead of people — do repetitive and lower-value work, such as logging into applications and systems, moving files and folders, extracting, copying, and inserting data, filling in forms, and completing routine analyses and reports. Advanced bots can even perform cognitive processes, such as interpreting text, engaging in chats and conversations, understanding unstructured data, and applying advanced machine learning models to make complex decisions.

Harness Consumer Insights for Decision-Making

Companies can use customer insights to inform decision-making. For example, retailers can use AI to access and analyze available information related to customer preferences, choice, and purchase history to better understand and predict consumer behavior. Predictive analysis driven by AI could allow retailers to provide customized recommendations to encourage spending and repeat purchases. Websites can also install automated processes that use deep analytics to analyze customer behavior and browsing history to enhance consumer experiences by providing suggestions on what users want to view or purchase.

Netflix is famous for using AI to show its users tailored recommendations on what to view and when to view them, but this technology can naturally be leveraged by smaller companies as well. These digital processes free up resources as companies no longer need to track consumer behavior manually or through market surveys. This asynchronous form of consumer research provides companies with richer data to make business decisions. By receiving information on whether a product is in high demand based on consumer browsing history, a company can decide if it should provide a certain type of offering or if it should discontinue it.

Customers also provide feedback through interactions with AI customer service chatbots. These chatbots can pick up emotions — joy, sadness, anger, and boredom, for instance — by analyzing texts sent by customers. ParallelDots, a medium-sized AI company, has an Emotion Analysis Application Programming Interface (API) that specializes in categorizing text into six different emotions, trained on their dataset. By understanding customers' pain points, companies can take a more proactive approach to creating more business opportunities. Instead of being reactive (i.e., by responding to customer complaints), firms can use these insights to understand underlying factors, prioritize to solve root causes of issues faced by customers, and be at the front line of customer experiences to increase customer loyalty for more sustainable growth.

Improve Internal Business Operations for Efficiency and Sustainability

Businesses can also use AI to improve and streamline internal business operations in a bid to pursue sustainability goals. Through a process called business lifecycle analysis, companies can perform a systematic and holistic review of their value chain, quantifying the environmental impacts related to all stages of the lifecycle of the manufacturing of products. AI can be used to calculate energy use, greenhouse gas emissions, carbon footprint, process efficiency, and throughput. Companies can use data loggers, which are essentially electronic devices that can monitor and record specific parameters (e.g., energy usage) over time. By understanding and capturing data corresponding to energy consumption across various processes within the lifecycle, companies can recognize parts where they can reduce energy consumption and identify sources where they can reduce waste.

When Ray Anderson, CEO of Interface, a global carpet manufacturer, embarked on the company's sustainability journey in the 1990s, the first challenge he wanted to overcome in his bid to climb "Mount Sustainability" was to eliminate waste. Between 1996 and 2013, Interface reduced the manufacturing waste it sent to landfills by 84%. By using technology to track and analyze waste, the total energy use at the factories reduced by 39% per unit, and 7 out of 9 facilities started operating with 100% renewable energy.[8] While Interface is a larger global business, smaller companies can emulate this, and use technological innovations to their advantage.

Technology Opportunities for SMEs

Higher Agility

Indeed, SMEs are more agile and adaptive to leverage newer technologies to achieve their goals. To automate processes, harness consumer insights, and conduct business lifecycle analysis, company data must be gathered and stored in a common space. Full data transparency is pivotal for AI to be most effective, as learning from incomplete or biased data leads to different conclusions for managerial decision-making.

This is where smaller companies possess competitive advantage because compared to larger firms, it is easier for smaller companies to coordinate digitalization and storage of data for AI purposes. First, processes and information related to these processes are fewer and less complex compared to large firms. Second, there tend to be fewer legacy systems — outdated systems, technology, or software applications that were initially used for functions that may now be obsolete. This translates into less effort in changing these systems and in converting and storing data to a format that can be analyzed by machine learning. Third, there are fewer stakeholders to manage in the process of obtaining information from all departments in the company. Fourth, stakeholders or employees involved in the provision of data for AI also tend to be more vested in the success of the company, and this digital transformation journey tends to be smoother for SMEs than for larger bureaucratic corporations.

Family-like Culture as an Advantage

Employees of SMEs tend to be more aligned with the organizational mission and are more loyal to the company compared to employees of larger firms, due to a more family-like organizational culture present in smaller firms and closeness to leadership when it comes to decision-making. With recent research showing that some employees may choose to withhold information to gain individual advantage related to performance and promotion opportunities, a family-like culture as in SMEs is beneficial in countering this and promoting data transparency. For instance, Harvard Business Review reported that 60% of employees have a problem getting information they need from their colleagues.[9] This phenomenon tends to occur less frequently in smaller companies, where there are higher levels of trust among co-workers, higher psychological safety, and higher alignment of employees' values to those of the organization. The move toward information and data transparency can thus be executed faster in small companies to leverage AI and technology.

Leveraging Existing Innovations through Networks

SMEs should also be aware that they do not have to create these software platforms from scratch. Recognizing that they have access to fewer resources to invest in R&D and digital innovation, what some SMEs have done successfully is to use their current networks to gain access to AI solutions. For instance, Dorfner, a medium-sized German industrial minerals company, tapped into a preexisting AI platform for chemicals from its network in Silicon Valley. Dorfner used this AI technology to run simulations for its formulations, subsequently offering a new sustainable formulation service for its clients.[10] In India, small and medium-sized banks can take advantage of an AI-powered conversational banking platform FinoAllied. It comes with built-in banking services and transactions which can be integrated with the various digital channels of these Indian banks to be offered to customers.[11]

It is important to note that tapping into present networks is different from simply "buying" digital solutions as highlighted earlier in this chapter. This situation is unlike, say, Facebook acquiring Instagram or the U.S.-based talent evaluation company SHL acquiring HR tech start-up Aspiring Minds for its job credentialing platform. It is about SMEs seeking solutions which are in line with fulfilling their technology objectives, without infusing those innovations as part of their portfolio. Similar to how smaller companies mobilize their networks to receive financial and non-financial support for growth and in times of crises, SMEs can reach out to the networks they are embedded in to share information and solutions.

Start Small

Radical change can be — and often is — easier to execute in smaller firms. What is key to recognize here, however, is that smaller firms do not have to embark on transformational journeys or enact radical change to take advantage of digitalization and AI. There are opportunities for them to look inward into their existing business processes and identify where they can implement technology and AI to pursue long-term financial growth and sustainability goals. Without expending significant resources on inventing new innovations, SMEs can utilize their current strengths in being nimble, having a committed workforce, and tapping into their preexisting networks to use AI to streamline their current processes, and pivot to be more digitally ready.

Risks Associated with AI

Cybersecurity

New technologies do not come without risks. To maximize the potential of algorithms and machine learning for data-driven decision-making, full data transparency is needed. Especially when SMEs utilize free or low-cost open software or cloud platforms, their data become more vulnerable to cyberattacks. With increased digitalization that allows employees to work from anywhere, connecting to work-related matters using insecure networks could lead to important company and/or consumer data being compromised.

According to recent reports, small businesses are three times more likely to be targeted by cybercriminals than larger companies. Barracuda Networks, a cloud security company, analyzed millions of emails across thousands of companies in 2021. They found that, on average, an employee of a company with fewer than 100 personnel will experience 350% more social engineering attacks compared to an employee of a large enterprise.[12] In a survey conducted by the Singapore Business Federation (SBF), 60% of all cyberattacks were on small businesses.

SMEs are often prime targets as they tend to lack the required resources and premium protection to minimize their exposure to cyberattacks and malware. In the survey by SBF, the most prevalent types of cyberattacks were business email scams and ransomware attacks. These not only resulted in financial losses but also affected employee productivity and efficiency.[13]

There are several reasons why SMEs are more vulnerable to cybersecurity threats. First, employees are insufficiently informed on cybersecurity issues. Many employees do not know about phishing scams, and lean operations in smaller businesses often mean that insufficient time and attention is given to training employees on identifying and avoiding cyber threats. Indeed, according to a recent Harvard Business Review article, human error is the biggest threat to cybersecurity, accounting for 80% of such incidents.[14] Unintentional actions (such as clicking on a phishing link) or a lack of action (such as not changing a weak password) can cause or allow security breaches to occur.

Second, smaller companies have weaker IT infrastructure and support. As mentioned earlier, SMEs tend to have lower levels of digital infrastructure. Defending against complex cybersecurity threats also requires a dedicated team or individual ensuring that the network and devices in the organization are not vulnerable or compromised. Smaller companies simply do not have the capacity to hire personnel to fulfill data security roles, as described earlier.

To overcome issues related to cybersecurity, SMEs need to first be aware that resources need to be dedicated to infrastructure, personnel, and training to ensure that members of the organization are ready against potential attacks. While limited resources might hinder smaller companies from having full-time employees or a dedicated team for this, they could start by hiring a part-time employee or by including data security officer roles in the official job description as part of a myriad of roles held by an employee — as opposed to having an ad-hoc arrangement and handling cybersecurity issues only "as and when" company networks and data are compromised. This should be part of an overall data readiness strategy. Data readiness refers to a company's state of preparedness to collect, process, and analyze data to create organizationally valued outcomes. Before being able to process and analyze data to make optimal business decisions, SMEs should ensure that the correct data protection policies are in place and that employees are well trained.

To increase data readiness levels, SMEs can also benefit from engaging in multi-stakeholder collaborations. For example, regular engagement with municipalities and governmental bodies allows SMEs to remain up to date with the latest local regulations with respect to data security. This additionally gives them a platform to raise concerns to local authorities, given that smaller companies are more vulnerable to cyberattacks. This could in turn motivate lawmakers to implement regulations to protect consumers and companies, instead of placing the responsibility solely on companies — where larger corporations are advantaged. Collaboration with non-governmental organizations, academia, as well as grassroots organizations could also result in programs to promote data regulation awareness and literacy.[15]

Ethical Concerns: Data Protection and Privacy

There are several ethical concerns related to utilizing AI including, but not limited to, data protection, data privacy, transparency, reproducibility, and bias. Where the rate of innovation is faster than regulations, data privacy can be an issue. Companies may collect consumer data such as name, age, gender, ethnicity, and education background to profit from processing and analyzing such data. For instance, by understanding the demographic profile of individuals making purchases on a shopping website, advertisements and products can be customized to target this particular group. These websites may require customers to input personal data in online forms upon purchase. As mentioned earlier, this saves the company resources in conducting market surveys and also time as the data are captured in real time. Furthermore, other types of data like clicks, shopping preferences, device specifications, location, and search history are collected by tracking cookies. A cookie ID, the identifier included in most cookies when set on a user's browser which remembers the individual's preferences and settings, is also considered personal data.

The issue arises when consumers are not aware that their data are being collected in the background, and without explicit consent from users, it is questionable for companies to collect and use the data — especially when they are making financial profit from this information. In the European Union (EU), the General Data Protection Regulation (GDPR) attempts to overcome this by setting strict laws on data collection and by adopting the broadest interpretation of "personal data" as possible. Under the GDPR, consumers have greater control on which type of personal data they release to businesses, if they wish to release them at all.

The GDPR provides individuals with more control over their personal data by requiring data protection (ensuring businesses keep data secure) and data privacy (ensuring that people can exercise their right to privacy).[16] Where the EU adopts blanket regulations for the whole of the European Union, Africa takes a more sovereign approach, where African countries can choose to be part of a data protection regulation network. Currently, 36 out of 54 African countries have data protection laws and/or regulations. 16 countries have signed the African Union Convention on Cyber Security and Personal Data Protection ("Malabo Convention") and 13 countries have ratified it.[17]

Despite these regulations to ensure data protection and data privacy, some services and products *require* users to provide personal data in order to have the right to use these services. For example, Facebook requires users to agree to their version of data protection policies (which may not provide individuals much protection at all). Otherwise, they do not have user access to the platform. Recently, Facebook removed several information fields from user profiles, including religious and political views.[18] Despite these fields being removed, and some users wanting to be discreet about their religious and political views, algorithms based on users' "likes" and preferences allow Facebook to make deductions about individuals' views. The data are valuable as advertisers, including many political campaigns, may pay Facebook to show their ads to specific demographic groups.[19]

While users currently have lower bargaining power in protecting their personal data, there is increasing pressure on companies to collect and use data more responsibly, as evident by the proceedings against Facebook and TikTok for their data privacy violations.[20] Small and medium-sized enterprises need to be prepared to be affected by potential, more restrictive, regulations that arise out of these concerns, and ensure that there are sufficient technological and human systems in place for corresponding compliance.

Ethical Concerns: Bias due to Historical Data

Another major ethical concern of using AI is in the bias present in input data. As AI learns from past decisions, implicit biases may be carried forward in algorithms. An experiment conducted by Johns Hopkins University and Georgia Institute of Technology is a prime example on how human biases could translate to discriminatory behaviors by robots. In this experiment, robots were presented with blocks with pictures of individuals and were to assign these blocks titles, such as "doctor", "criminal", "homemaker", and "janitor". Researchers tracked the frequency at which the AI robots assigned these titles to varying genders and races. Compared to White men, Black men were 10% more likely to be identified as "criminals" and Latino men were 10% more likely to be identified as "janitors". They responded to words like "homemaker" and "janitor" by choosing blocks with women and people of color, and women of all ethnicities were also less likely to be identified as "doctor".[21] These decisions were made based on the current gender and ethnicity makeup in these titles, in which much bias and history are embedded.

There are understandably concerns that these biases are present in recruitment in businesses. If an HR officer enters the gender, ethnicity, educational background, religion, and sexual orientation of past employees as part of input data for AI-driven recruitment decisions, bias that may be present in past human decisions is not only brought forward but may even be exacerbated through AI. Prior to the application of AI, multiple studies had already found that applicants were less likely to be called for interviews if their names gave clues to the fact that they belonged to a disadvantaged group or ethnicity.

For example, in 2001, researchers at the National Bureau of Economic Research sent fictitious resumes with either African American-sounding (such as Lakisha or Jamal) or White-sounding (such as Emily Walsh and Greg Baker) names in response to help-wanted advertisements in Chicago and Boston newspapers and measured the number of callbacks each resume received for interviews. The research team responded to more than 1,300 employment ads in the sales, administrative support, clerical, and customer services job categories, sending out nearly 5,000 resumes. Controlling for qualifications, job applicants with White names needed to send about 10 resumes to get one callback; those with African American names needed to send around 15 resumes to get one callback, resulting in a 50% difference.[22]

Almost two decades later, this study and its findings were replicated by economists from UC Berkeley and the University of Chicago. They sent more than 83,000 fictitious applications with randomized characteristics to geographically dispersed jobs posted by 108 of the largest U.S. employers. They found that distinctively Black names reduced the probability of employer contact by 2.1 percentage points relative to distinctively White names. The effect was particularly greater in 23 Fortune 500 employers, which established systemic discrimination in hiring practices.[23] A 2016 study in Malaysia utilizing a similar methodology also found discrimination in hiring between resumes with Chinese names and Malay names.[24]

When human recruiters are unable to make perfect decisions due to inherent biases, bounded rationality, and an inexplicable "gut feel", replicating those flawed decisions using AI can threaten societal progress. To ensure that companies are future-ready by embracing policies and practices to increase diversity, equity, and inclusion, we need to be mindful of the kind of historical data inputted into AI algorithms. Do these data points reflect our inherent biases? Are the decisions as a result of AI ethical? Are the algorithms transparent, reproducible, and responsible?

AI is definitely here to stay for a long time. While we can (and should) embrace AI to focus on the opportunities as mentioned earlier, we should also be wary of allowing AI to make important decisions and ensure that they are in line with our sustainability goals.

Case Study: AI in Recruitment

Although we discussed earlier that AI can replicate and exacerbate human biases, two rising companies in Singapore, Pulsifi and Careera, show us that we can use AI to *remove* biases. Both companies use AI technology to predict job candidates who are the best fit for specific job roles. Using scores from personality and cognitive assessments, together with their clients' success profiles, these companies use machine learning and customized algorithms to find the best talent fit for their client. In Pulsifi, these different facets of a candidate are combined with data from automated CV analysis and skills assessments, and computed to form one comprehensive "Fit Score".[25]

Careera helps companies hire better, faster, and fairer. Hiring companies can list a job on Careera, as well as on other job boards, and potential candidates will then use the Careera app to upload their resume and go through several bite-sized assessments. Instead of receiving hundreds of applicants, a hiring company will get a shortlist of up to ten candidates who are a good fit for the job. Careera uses AI throughout this process, such as when taking information from a CV, when listing a job, and when matching candidates to jobs. This provides much higher accuracy than traditional keyword search — and there is no application process that the candidate must go through. Using a user-friendly interface, candidates swipe left or right on a particular posting on the app: candidates swipe right on a posting they are interested in and left on those that they are not. If the employer agrees that this is a good match, they can set up an interview right away. Both companies provide CV screening services through automation, and identifiable information such as name, gender, age, ethnicity, and other distinguishable features are not shared with employers during these matching stages.

There are benefits to using AI and automation for hiring. First, it saves HR managers significant man-hours in going through CVs manually and calling in candidates for face-to-face interviews. According to *Zapier*, a task automation company based in the U.S., automation saves HR professionals 8 hours per week.[26] Second, it increases predictive accuracy as it uses and learns from tens of thousands of data points to identify an ideal candidate using job success factors, relying less on human gut feel. Third, bias is reduced in the application process, as recruiters evaluate candidates based on their calculated Fit Scores, or on whether there is a "match", without looking at cues that give away candidates' gender, ethnicity, and nationality (e.g., names).

Indeed, Pulsifi reported over 90% accuracy in hiring decisions, as validated by job performance. Their innovation also resulted in fairer opportunities for candidates and greater gender diversity in the pool of shortlisted candidates when their platform was used, compared to prior cohorts. "Pulsifi's vision is to help people and organizations achieve their potential. We want to impact as many people as possible around the world, so we leverage AI technology in order to scale quickly," said Jay Huang, CEO and co-founder of Pulsifi. On top of matching and growing the right people in the right roles in companies, Pulsifi also pursues sustainability through stronger governance by "improving employees' skills and job satisfaction, and stronger governance with explainable people decisions and succession plans, and privacy and security of people data".

At Careera, the founders place SDGs that they pursue at the forefront. On the company website, Careera commits to SDG 5: Gender Equality, SDG 8: Decent Work and Economic Growth, SDG 9: Industry, Innovation, and Infrastructure, SDG 10: Reduced Inequalities, and SDG 11: Sustainable Cities and Communities as core features, with five other SDGs as supporting measures. With the belief that "building an ethical business isn't optional", Careera also plans to pursue B Corp certification as a testament to its commitment to sustainability.[27]

Despite the companies' best efforts at anonymizing candidates' data, *some* amount of bias may still exist, as decisions made past the interview stage are still largely determined by human recruiters. This is due to the fact that some candidate skills are best presented face to face, such as in-person communication, professionalism, and performance under pressure. Bridging the best of both worlds, at the present moment, "co-AI" — a joint approach of decision-making between humans and AI — is touted as the optimal style of decision-making.

Digital Infrastructure and Societal Impact

So, how do technology and digital infrastructure play a role in SMEs' societal impact? Analyzing the sample of 773 SMEs and mid-sized companies across the globe in 2021 and 2022, I examined the relationships of digital infrastructure on the three pillars of company future readiness: long-term financial growth, societal impact, and adaptive capacity. After controlling for region, industry, revenue, and number of full-time employees, regression analyses showed that out of business orientation, business model, networks, and digital infrastructure, *digital infrastructure* had the largest impact on overall future readiness (β = .314, p < .01) out of these four predictors (Figure 1). The effect of digital infrastructure on societal impact (β = .222, p < .01) specifically is also about double compared to the effect of business orientation (β = .100, p < .01) and business model

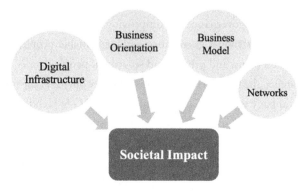

Figure 1.   *Effects of digital infrastructure, business orientation, business model, and networks on societal impact dimension of future readiness.*

(β = .119, p < .01), and four times higher than the role of networks (β = .048, p < .01).

What this means is that firms with higher levels of digital infrastructure in this research study created greater societal impact. They reported higher levels of engagement with government bodies on identifying how they can best support efforts to achieve the Sustainable Development Goals (SDGs), develop specific outcome indicators to measure the company's positive contributions to the SDGs, and define targets for these outcome indicators in line with their respective national development strategy. They also reported having higher levels of incorporation of social and environmental consideration in their performance and strategy compared to their competitors.

One Strategy, Two Goals: Using Technology for Sustainability

These findings highlight the enormous opportunity for businesses to engage in a "twin transformation" approach of leveraging technology to not only increase the company's competitive advantage amidst the technological noise but also solve problems related to sustainability such as climate change, poverty, and social inequality. Indeed, leading sustainability experts at McKinsey say that technological innovations *shape* the global sustainability agenda.[28] For example, public electric vehicles (EVs) — 300,000 electric buses are in use in

China's public transportation — help eliminate emissions of greenhouse gases while saving costs on diesel. Technology available to capture and store carbon emissions also helps to significantly reduce greenhouse gas emissions, while using the captured carbon dioxide to other revenue-generating ventures, such as manufacturing plastics which can subsequently be recycled.

As highlighted earlier, SMEs can use AI to analyze sources of inefficiency in business processes to reduce energy and resource consumption, greenhouse gas emissions, and waste generation of products and services during a product's lifecycle. This would first require SMEs to digitalize their processes, bearing in mind data transparency and other concerns with regard to quality of data as highlighted earlier. The data-driven green decision-making that results from this helps smaller companies keep track of their impact on the environment. Organizations can use technology to assess their current state of sustainable practices and create a corresponding road map to achieve sustainability goals. By identifying sources of inefficiencies and waste, SMEs can optimize business processes to reduce their carbon footprint — and the savings incurred can be subsequently invested in value-generating sustainable strategies.

Case Study: Kuza

An example of an SME successfully leveraging technology for societal impact is Kuza. Kuza is a women-run B Corp-certified social enterprise from Kenya. Focusing on the "bottom billion", Kuza offers a mobile-first micro-learning platform that provides youth, women, and micro-entrepreneurs from informal communities with opportunities to learn, connect, and grow. By ideating and executing structured learning programs, Kuza's educational tools for members of the agricultural and rural communities aim to help them transform their businesses on their own terms and at their own convenience. To date, Kuza's innovations have impacted over 6 million people.

Kuza uses technology to create meaningful networks to benefit society. In Kenya, the average age of the Kenyan farmer is 60 years. Kuza reaches out to this demographic by engaging local youths as transformation agents, who teach the older farmers how to use Kuza's micro-learning platform and digital tools. By sharing knowledge at the grassroots level, these younger individuals "handhold" some of these elders to understand how to use digital devices and access e-learning resources to bridge the knowledge gap of a population that previously had little or no access to such technology.

Despite using technology to create a positive societal impact, Kuza understands the limitations of the local infrastructure in connecting to the Internet, especially in rural areas where the farmers live. According to founder and chief mentor Sriram Bharatam, "The communities who are at the bottom billion are not completely connected to the Internet, and also majority of them are not even connected to power. We engage them using a set of exponential technologies and digital technologies. We do that fundamentally by creating youth-led entrepreneurs from remote communities, and have a thorough process of incubating them, called Rural Entrepreneur Development Incubators (REDI). Then, we give them a portable digital backpack, which is designed to work off-grid without Internet."

As a result, an independent study done on Kuza farmers in 2022 by the World Bank in Kenya and AgriFin reported that 97% of farmers experienced an improvement in their overall quality of life because of Kuza. By creating an ecosystem comprising youths and mentors who provide emotional, functional, and technical support to micro-entrepreneurs, Kuza's work impacts 10 UN SDGs[29] as this SME hopes to drive a global movement, providing a collective voice to millions of individuals previously excluded from important conversations.

Technology as a Means to an End: Vision Comes First

There is huge potential in leveraging technology for positive impact on the environment and the society. However, what the abovementioned figures also show is that companies with less digital infrastructure (i.e., smaller companies) create less societal impact. While these figures fall in line with the "reality" of small companies — small companies' level of societal impact is below average and falls behind that of bigger businesses — this does not have to be the case. It has been shown earlier that pivoting to digital transformation and sustainability is *easier* for smaller companies, and digital innovations can be scaled at relatively low cost. So, what can SMEs do in light of this finding?

The answer lies in creating and maintaining a company *vision* that marries technology and societal impact. Going back to the case study on Kuza, Bharatam believes that people, trust, and a strong purpose are what come first. "We are a strong believer of the fact that one plus one is 11. When you bring tools to partners together with a common, shared vision and values, you can create magic and everything that we have done is a true testimony of that." While Kuza indeed leverages technology in its business model, Bharatam explains, "People, process, and technology, are the three cornerstones on which you can actually build the future readiness of a company. People, where I mean all actors, and the way they come together in the process is where we can make a collective difference. Technology is just a means to an end." Technology plays a facilitative role, but a strong vision is at the core.

A vision refers to a strong mental picture of a desired future state. It represents an alluring ideal future that is credible, yet not immediately attainable. According to Stanford business professors Jim Collins and Jerry Porras, good visions are widely shared, optimistic, unique, future-oriented, and visual (i.e., can be pictured).[30] In future-ready companies, a strong vision is one that is ambitious and challenges members of the organization. What is needed is "such a big commitment that when people see what the goal will take, there's almost an audible gulp".[31] It is important for founders and leaders to understand the core ideology of the company and to communicate that core ideology to the rest of the organization. Instead of jumping onto the latest bandwagon of technological trends — which smaller companies cannot afford to do anyway — SMEs should look inward, focus on their vision and core purpose, and leverage technology to achieve that.

Remember, technology and innovation look different in different times. For cavemen, *fire* was considered technology. For us today, technology is represented by robots and digitalization. For a company to be future-ready, the business model cannot collapse if the technology takes on a different form.

With a strong vision, leaders can understand that the *way* to get to a vision might require adaptability and agility, but the *core ideology* remains steadfast. Digital readiness and the presence of good digital infrastructure may help SMEs survive in a fast-paced environment, but with a good set of people to help leaders achieve the company vision, technology is best used as a means to an end.

Part Four

People as an Asset

Chapter 6

The 3 Rs of Talent: Resourcefulness, Resilience, and Right for the Company

Apart from concerns related to survival and expansion, talent acquisition and retention were cited as top challenges faced by small and medium-sized enterprises. According to the global SME study I ran with the World Economic Forum, 48% of companies surveyed cited *talent* as a major challenge in 2022, at a similar level to the previous year of 52.5%. With the Great Resignation waves in 2021 and 2022, it becomes even more crucial for companies to provide employees with environments that allow them to thrive and encourage them to stay. Coupled with the fact that the average training cost per employee is highest among smaller companies, SME decision makers need to be mindful with their talent acquisition and retention strategies. How can they attract and retain talent in order to be future-ready?

Although larger companies tend to spend more resources on training and development of employees, training costs per employee are higher in small companies when the total is averaged out. For example, in Europe, small companies spend only 1.5% of labor expenditures on employee training compared to the average of 2.3%. In Australia, only a third of small companies provide organized training for employees, as opposed to 70% in medium-sized enterprises and 98% among large organizations.[1] However, due to their comparative disadvantage with regard to economies of scale, training costs per employee are higher in SMEs. In 2021, large companies with over 10,000 employees spent US$722 per employee, whereas small companies spent an average of US$1,433 per employee.[2] When turnover happens, especially when an employee quits within six months or less after receiving training, labor costs to hire and retrain become very expensive.

The Great Resignation: Expectations from Employees

What is the Great Resignation? This trend received much attention in early 2021, in the wake of the COVID-19 pandemic. Essentially, it refers to the voluntary resignation of employees en masse, sometimes without the prospect of a new job at the time of resignation. According to the U.S. Bureau of Labor Statistics, 47.7 million Americans voluntarily quit their jobs in 2021[3] — an unprecedented mass exit from the workforce. In 2022, 50.6 million U.S. workers left their jobs.[4]

The Great Resignation trend was not confined to the United States. Microsoft ran a global study for their Work Trend Index Annual Report 2022 with 31,000 people from 31 countries covering North America, Latin America, Asia and Pacific Islands, Europe, Australia, and New Zealand, with similar findings.[5] Globally, 17% of employees left their jobs in 2020, with the trend increasing to 18% in 2021. Turnover intention was particularly high among the younger workforce, with 52% of Gen Z and Millennials likely to consider changing employers in the year of the study.

Compared to before the pandemic, employees now have a new "worth it" equation. According to the 2022 Work Trend Index, 47% were more likely to put family and personal life over work than they were two years earlier, and 53% of employees were more likely to prioritize health and well-being over work than before the pandemic. These echo the main reasons employees quit in 2020 and 2021. The top five reasons cited were personal well-being or mental health (24%), work-life balance (24%), risk of getting COVID-19 (21%), lack of confidence in senior management or leadership (21%), and lack of flexible hours or location (21%).

Employee priorities have significantly shifted when it comes to what is important at the workplace. Previously, employees intended to quit when they faced job stressors, characterized by high levels of attention required by their jobs, high role demands, pressure to complete tasks, time urgency, and heavy workloads.[6] In particular, when they did not receive sufficient organizational resources in terms of support and training, and when they perceived role ambiguity and role conflict in their job, employees experienced lower levels of satisfaction with their jobs, had lower commitment to their company, and

subsequently voluntarily left. This is concerning because it tends to be the good performers who leave the company, when employees experience low levels of job satisfaction and organizational support.[7]

Quiet Quitting

Closely related to the Great Resignation, another trend worth noting is "quiet quitting". This refers to the behavior of individuals who retain an employment status with the company, but are psychologically disconnected from their employer. Some examples of behaviors representative of quiet quitting are putting in the minimum amount of effort required, leaving work on time, and opting out of tasks beyond one's assigned scope of duties. According to Gallup's State of the Global Workplace Report 2023, 59% of the global workforce engage in quiet quitting, with the highest percentage in Europe at 72%.[8] Gallup estimates that quiet quitting costs the global economy US$8.8 trillion and accounts for 9% of global GDP. Leadership directly influences engagement levels of these employees, and the later sections in this chapter as well as this book discuss this.

In the current labor environment, it is apparent that employees' intention to quit goes beyond factors directly related to the job such as salary, working hours, training needed to perform their roles effectively, and promotion and career development. Mental health and well-being are at the forefront. Depression, anxiety, and burnout at the workplace increasingly need to be addressed,[9] and suicide risk among the youth (Gen Z workforce) is at an all-time high.[10–12] Organizations need to provide an environment that fosters autonomy and flexibility for employees to perform their tasks at a location and timing of their choice, with care for their interests outside of work (as personal spheres and family become more important consideration factors for workers), all while ensuring that individuals thrive mentally and emotionally.

There were several arguments that the Great Resignation trend occurred because of the onset of COVID-19, with employees embracing the importance of time with their loved ones and realizing that they could work remotely, and could thus relocate to more affordable cities. Despite these arguments, several scholars pointed out that when analyzing average monthly resignation data from 2009 through 2019 and forecasting those figures to 2021, voluntary turnover has been increasing steadily by 0.10 percentage points each year, and that this trend has been happening since before COVID-19.[13] Nonetheless, what remains clear is that now employees have higher — and very different — expectations of their jobs, leaders, and the working environment. With the opportunity costs higher for smaller companies in this situation, SMEs need unique strategies to keep up.

Expectations from Employers

The challenges related to talent do not only revolve around demands from employees. Employers are also finding it difficult to find talent that fulfill requirements for job vacancies. According to LinkedIn figures, some sectors which are growing in terms of job opportunities are Technology and IT, Cyber Security, Sustainability and Environment, and Insight and Analytics.[14] Some skills that will be needed in the future are artificial intelligence (AI) and machine learning, data science and analytics, blockchain, robotics and automation, and deep knowledge on sustainability — some of which did not exist as recently as five years ago.

The demand for talent to fill in new roles — such as Chief Information Security Officer managing security policies to protect critical data and Chief Sustainability Officer championing a company's sustainability efforts to fulfill ESG goals — is increasing. Yet, formalized training and higher educational degrees to produce talent with these hard skills are uncommon, not as well established, and institutions themselves are trying to keep up with certifications required by the market and regulators.

This trend will increase in the future as critical skills needed in the job market can only be *newly* acquired due to technological and educational constraints. At present, job candidates equipped with the "right" technical skills, such as coding and machine learning, are rare in a pool highly demanded by employers. SMEs with lesser ability to offer an attractive remuneration package naturally lose out to their MNC competitors in the war for talent in this aspect. Getting creative in their recruitment strategies is one way to gain a competitive advantage.

In developed countries, high labor costs also put local SMEs at a disadvantage. Job candidates based in these countries often turn down offers from SMEs in favor of a higher pay package or a more reputable, bigger company. In a tech SME based in Singapore which I interviewed, the acceptance rate of job offers was as low as 30%.

At Responsible Cyber, a boutique Singapore-headquartered cybersecurity and risk management company building a third-party risk management product, called IMMUNE X-TPRM, Dr. Magda Lilia Chelly, the co-founder and managing director, delved into the hurdles her company encountered when seeking senior software engineers. Many potential candidates were pushing for salaries that surpassed the firm's designated ranges. In response to such challenges, an increasing number of tech company founders, including those at Responsible Cyber, are turning their sights toward countries with more affordable labor costs. Not only do these candidates have ample training for the technical skills required for the job but they also incur lower costs for the company, as long as cross-border data flows are reliable and secure.

For example, Careera, an AI HR company based in Singapore, reported savings of US$28,800 per year for mid-level mobile developers and US$54,000 per year for senior developers, with both roles outsourced to Oman. These savings are calculated based on salary statistics for full-stack developers in Singapore from the 2023 Southeast Asia Startup Talent Report, and what the company will have otherwise paid.[15]

However, beyond technical skills, many of which only *recently* started flourishing as must-haves, employers are increasingly placing emphasis on soft skills such as adaptability, flexibility, and potential for leadership. With the onset of COVID-19, which saw changes in recruitment, decision-making, and ways of working, employers demand that their workers have the ability to be agile and keep up with the changes as seamlessly as possible. For example, workers had to quickly adapt to remote or hybrid work arrangements as the world went through various stages of lockdown in light of the pandemic. This not only required digital literacy to hold and attend meetings via video conferencing tools like Slack, Zoom, and Google Meets but also communication skills to convey messages effectively in a virtual setting.

> **Digital/Hybrid Work Arrangement**
>
> The younger workforce is an interesting group to take a closer look at in this regard. They are more digitally literate, having grown up with technological devices and using them for school, work, and play. However, they may find difficulty in persevering with the job as they attempt to cope with high levels of uncertainty. Sometimes dubbed the "strawberry generation",[a] resilience among the younger workforce is more sought after, as employers recognize that they need to recruit individuals who can adapt to and tide through multiple changes. Some employers also have concerns as to whether this generation that is used to virtual means of communication is able to convey messages effectively in a face-to-face setting, if they wish to return physically to work at all.

While hard skills and technical knowledge are not unimportant per se, employers and employees alike need a core set of soft skills, as they prepare for upskilling beyond their current set of degrees and specializations. This is when SMEs can use the principle of the 3 Rs in their talent acquisition and retention strategies: Resourcefulness, Resilience, and Right for the company.

1st R: Resourcefulness

Resourcefulness here refers to an individual's ability to utilize their current (limited) resources — financial, social, and informational — in a creative and agile way to achieve their objectives. Particularly for SMEs with fewer resources, this competency helps expand the company's ability to cope with internal and external challenges. With flexible alternatives to solve a problem, companies are in a better position to tackle issues in their daily business operations, especially in extremely difficult times. Resourcefulness comes in behaviors as simple as using a sugar packet to stabilize an unsteady table, to rebranding a product to target new customers. Collectively, these behaviors from employees lend the organization the agility to reconfigure and reallocate its resources, as well as redefine its existing business strategy.

---

[a] The "strawberry generation" is a term given to the younger generation, who is sometimes stereotyped to be less resilient, and like strawberries, tend to "bruise easily".

It is, however, difficult for employers to identify an individual's level of resourcefulness from a CV, and traditional interview questions may not test candidates on this aspect adequately. How can a company pick up on candidates' resourcefulness? How can one instill this in current employees? Through a case study of a science, technology, engineering, and math (STEM) offshoring firm, Sharesource, we see how a clear organizational vision of how the company's employees should be, together with ensuring cultural fit in the recruitment process, can create an environment that encourages resourcefulness.

Case Study: Sharesource

Founded in 2013, Sharesource is a global offshoring firm, specializing in the STEM field. Operating five team hubs based in Australia, the Philippines, Zimbabwe, Canada, and Vietnam, Sharesource matches remote tech workers in developing countries with global companies in a bid to equalize opportunities and provide meaningful work for STEM graduates. Sharesource is at the cusp of growth, boasting 70% growth over the past three years, and has 250 employees to date.

Its CEO, Brendon Boyce, recognizes that "talent can come from anywhere". With this in mind, the company set up offices in countries like the Philippines and Vietnam to build remote teams for smart people. Sharesource marries technology and resourceful talent to give opportunities to smart people across the globe by adapting the idea of offshore call centers to the company's business model.

Boyce was inspired by the story of a young lady who could not fulfill her full potential due to lack of access to resources. "I met this young lady who was doing basic data entry work and when I asked about her qualifications, she had a Bachelor of Science and Mathematics. That made my heart sink, and I thought, we have to do something with those really smart people." Sharesource leverages technological innovations such as ZingHR, GroveHR, Skype, Slack, Google, and Zoom to connect global talent to international companies, allowing individuals to work from anywhere. Sharesource also utilizes online applications in the recruitment process.

Sharesource believes that when it has a group of smart and resourceful people, it can solve most problems. As a small company with constant challenges, being nimble and resourceful are key. For instance, in the Philippines, when employees worked from home during the lockdown period of the pandemic, there were insufficient Internet dongles[b] bought and distributed to employees. Not knowing when the period of working from home would end, some employees ran out of Internet access.

Boyce recalled, "After a Telco engineer worked two weeks from home, I heard his Internet wasn't working. When I asked what was happening, he told me that he was currently borrowing his neighbor's Internet. He was actually sitting between his neighbor's house and his own. But then it started raining and he had to go inside, so he couldn't use the Internet anymore. That is my favorite story. There is practical implementation of adaptability at the individual level across the business, and that's just one story. There are many others."

Indeed, Sharesource values this "hustle factor" from employees, who remarkably remained productive during times of change. Boyce remarked, "We were lucky enough that the people who work for us were able to go and work from home and adapt their behavior. They still keep the productivity and have the smarts to do a good job, so we've grown during this period."

However, "luck" is less of a determining factor here compared to Sharesource's deliberate talent acquisition strategy. Various Glassdoor reviews revealed that applicants had at least one culture fit interview in the application process, irrespective of the job role that the candidate is interviewing for, be it a Customer Success Specialist, a Network Planner, or a Senior Software Engineer.[16] They were asked non-traditional interview questions to determine if their values and behaviors aligned with those of Sharesource. Sample questions were: "What is one word to describe you in your family members' eyes?", "Tell me about yourself that is not in your resume", and "How would you be able to handle challenges?" Despite the

---

[b] An Internet dongle is a small USB Internet device or modem that allows users to access 3G, 4G, or 5G data by plugging it into their computer.

relative difficulty of the interview process (3.16/5), job candidates report positive application experiences with Sharesource.[17]

This talent acquisition approach emphasizes that Sharesource searches beyond technical skills when hiring and actively filters applicants based on levels of resourcefulness and alignment to the company's vision. Among the company values are "be proactive", "create value", and "add fun, passion, and love".[18] Individuals who align with these values will need to show initiative, productivity, and high levels of engagement.

Sharesource is successful in doing this because it is small, and strategically so. It is committed to growing organically while retaining its ability to remain nimble. This way, Sharesource is able to influence its company culture strongly. Quick communication and a cohesive team in times of crises also mean that solutions can be executed quickly by a group of smart individuals, handpicked through a rigorous recruitment strategy.

2nd R: Resilience

To keep up with the constant changes in a VUCA environment, companies need to be able to buffer themselves against the negative effects of these changes before they are able to pause, recollect, and re-strategize. Logically, organizations cannot move forward with their revised strategies if they are not able to first absorb the immediate impact of an occurrence in their environment. For this, companies need to ensure that they are resilient enough to face challenges of the future.

Resilience refers to the ability to bounce back from adversity to maintain the *status quo*.[19] From an organizational perspective, resilience comes in the form of financial slack resources, with enough financial reserves to cope with exigencies of a crisis and hinder undesirable outcomes such as layoffs and downsizing, as well as non-financial slack resources, which can come in the form of relational reserves, such as reaching out to networks and mobilizing them to provide additional resources.

From a talent perspective, resilience refers to individuals' capacity to stay with the company in times of crises, and in the words of mathematical statistician Nassim Taleb, instead of breaking under pressure, become "anti-fragile" and grow stronger under stress.[20] Research has shown that when resilient individuals work cohesively together, the organization gains from group resilience dynamics and this adds on to its social slack resources.[21] With fewer financial resources, SMEs are more dependent on their social reserves, and having resilient employees boosts that significantly. Indeed, interviews with future-ready SMEs in this research reveal that executives often find their *employees* to be a source of resilience for the company in hard times. This is why identifying resilient individuals is important in the talent acquisition process for smaller companies.

Similar to resourcefulness, it is difficult for recruiters to pick out resilience from a resume or a candidate's past work titles. Instead, SMEs could incorporate resilience-related assessments in their recruitment process. This can come in the form of posing a challenge during a team simulation event in one of the interview rounds, as well as asking targeted questions. For example, at the Koblenz University of Applied Sciences in Germany, the Department of Languages and International Affairs asks international internship applicants to describe a failure they experienced recently and how they overcame it. Being a young student moving to another country for the first time, where the language and working environment may be unfamiliar, high levels of resilience are required for interns to overcome potential initial cultural shocks.

What is important to be successful in this interview process is not for candidates to list their past achievements, but to be able to admit their past mistakes, reflect on them, and show in tangible terms what they have learnt from that situation. For instance, when a particular marketing effort for a student club failed, one applicant understood that she did not put in enough time into researching for this campaign, and failed to engage the relevant university stakeholders to make the campaign a success. As a result, the student prioritized research and relationship management in the next round of publicity efforts.

It is important to not only identify resilient individuals to offer them employment but to also continue encouraging resilience after they have become members of the organization. Leaders can increase employee resilience in two ways. First, they should lead by example. This is because resilient leaders tend to view failures differently. Instead of being ashamed of failure, resilient decision makers tend to perceive setbacks as opportunities for future success. They are able to turn obstacles into challenges and are able to use disruptive events to reinforce relationships and garner social support.

Resilience can also be "contagious". When followers see that their leader is calm, cool, and collected during a crisis, these positive emotions can trickle down and also cause employees to feel positive emotions of calmness and an overall determination that "they can do it". There is plenty of research on emotional contagion, and one direct benefit of positive emotions is that it increases individuals' awareness and repertoire of thoughts and actions to draw from to solve problems that come one's way.[22]

Although individual resilience levels are largely dispositional and based on childhood experiences,[23] there is growing research that shows that resilience is a psychological process that can be learned.[24] The second way to encourage resilience among employees is to increase what we call psychological safety. Psychological safety refers to a belief that individuals will not be punished or humiliated for speaking up with ideas, questions, concerns, or mistakes, and that the team is safe for interpersonal risk-taking.[25] In the previous example of Koblenz University of Applied Sciences, mistakes are not only encouraged in the International Internship Program but are also celebrated. If one runs into a problem or makes a mistake, he or she is encouraged to openly discuss it with other interns. This encourages self-reflection at a young age, and team members are also able to collaborate on problem-solving and learn together.

When there is an organizational culture created where employees feel safe to make mistakes and learn from them, going through a crisis could feel like a routine problem-solving occurrence. Employees draw from their skill set in using adverse situations as a learning opportunity and, together with resourcefulness and agility in thinking of creative solutions, help SMEs ride out difficult times. Against the backdrop of the Great Resignation, having a resilient workforce who is loyal to a small company already strapped in terms of financial resources makes a significant difference in remaining future-ready.

3rd R: Right for the Company

As mentioned earlier, SMEs are unable to compete with their larger counterparts in offering generous monetary compensations. Employees who tend to take up job offers with SMEs also often do so for non-monetary reasons. Individuals who choose to work with smaller companies do so because their ideas tend to be received more openly; with a smaller group of stakeholders, there is higher propensity to experiment, they can expand their skill set by taking on multiple roles, and they have higher visibility at the workplace. In innovative teams in start-ups, being able to build a product from scratch can provide employees with great levels of satisfaction. In fact, according to research conducted by Gallup, the largest U.S. companies have the lowest levels of engagement, while businesses with fewer than 25 employees have the most engaged employees who are highly involved, enthusiastic, and help drive the company forward.[26]

This is plausibly due to employees in smaller companies placing higher importance on the subjective dimensions of job quality such as well-being, purpose, personal development, relationships, and mentoring opportunities, as compared to objective dimensions of job quality such as pay, working hours, occupational safety, and job security. This is not to say that the objective measures of job quality should not be present, but individuals seeking to find a job that provides them with a sense of purpose and belongingness tend to be attracted to roles in companies where they could have personal and professional growth.

My research shows that future-ready SMEs attract talent by appealing to a higher organizational vision and other values. They are first clear on the organizational vision and the values they espouse, and select and retain talent based on these values. Indeed, compared to larger organizations, small companies place significantly higher importance on talent *fit* in recruitment considerations.[27] Talent fit does not refer to having the most qualified candidate in terms of technical skills, but rather the alignment of values of the candidate with the organization as well as with the current members in the company. Someone with a high talent fit is passionate about the organization's mission and is committed to helping achieve that mission by embodying the company values. In the instance of Sharesource, someone with a high talent fit is proactive, passionate, and works well with others in the team.

The 2022 study by World Economic Forum with over 400 SMEs worldwide found talent fit to be a significant predictor of all three pillars of future readiness:

long-term growth (β = .145, p < .05), societal impact (β = .271, p < .01), and adaptive capacity (β = .261, p < .01). This shows at a macro level how crucial it is for SMEs to hire, fire, and promote based on their company's core values in ensuring that the organization has a united workforce to increase its future readiness. When employees fit into the organizational culture, they work more cohesively together toward company goals with a common objective and fewer value-based conflicts.

In SMEs, executives have unique priorities when it comes to talent-related decisions. There are indeed several, more senior, roles where technical expertise is required, and those should be prioritized. Attracting such talent with objective measures of job quality may be needed. However, fewer resources also mean that SMEs may not be able to offer comparable compensation packages to more junior hires. They may need to be more open to hiring less-qualified people who demand a lower compensation package, and provide on-the-job training instead. This is driven by the belief that hard skills can be trained, whereas talent fit may be harder to come by.

Hiring people who are right for the company proves to be an important asset for SMEs, to the point where it can be a competitive advantage. According to Sriram Bharatam, founder of Kenyan-based agritech company Kuza, what sets the company apart from others is the people's mindset. "We are a strong believer of the fact that one plus one is 11. When you bring tools to partners together with a common, shared vision and values, you can create magic."

Having a mission which employees and leaders can embark on together helps build cohesive relationships, fosters trust and collaboration, and can increase group resilience as highlighted earlier. The resultant "family-like" culture also increases employee loyalty when the company is going through adversity. Most of the founders of future-ready SMEs whom I spoke to mentioned that their employees not only stayed with the company during the pandemic and worked doubly hard to get out of the dire situation together but some, such as in the case of Pulsifi, a Singapore-based AI company, also offered to forgo part of their salary to help the company stay afloat. This example further shows that when companies hire and promote passionate individuals who are committed to the organizational mission, they bullet-proof themselves to face present and future obstacles.

To assess alignment with the organizational vision, companies could include psychometric tests in the talent acquisition process such as the Organizational Culture Profile developed by O'Reilly and colleagues.[28] Some characteristics included in this assessment are being competitive, highly organized, adaptable, fair, analytical, and team-oriented. Arguably, candidates could choose to answer this assessment in a socially desirable manner, in spite of instructions to be honest when responding to the items. Thus, companies could complement this assessment by utilizing situational judgment tests (SJTs).

In an SJT, candidates are presented with a situation and multiple options on how to handle the situation, with no clear right answer. To assess integrity, for example, candidates will be presented with an ethical dilemma and asked how they will respond to that situation. For instance, a colleague currently placed on a Personal Improvement Plan is anxious about losing his job and passed off the candidate's idea as his own during a company-wide meeting. This colleague is also a good personal friend of the candidate, and the evaluation of the idea is team-based. This means that the entire team will be rewarded for the idea, not just this one colleague. What would the candidate do? Will the candidate speak up during the meeting, speak to the colleague privately, or bring this up to the manager? All responses in this case are logical options available to an individual, who may choose to follow one action over the other due to reasons grounded in personal principles and social norms. With no obvious right answer, but with an idea of what the code of conduct should be as per the organization's values, recruiters can assess if a candidate fits into the organizational culture based on the candidate's responses to the SJT.

This practice of choosing those who are Right for the company comes at an opportune time where workers' priorities have shifted as per the Great Resignation. Workers, especially the younger workforce, actively seek out jobs that provide them with self-fulfillment and meaning, and SMEs provide exactly that. Appealing to a grander vision to attract and retain talent is a strategy that SMEs have engaged in long before the pandemic, and now smaller companies are at an advantage as they are more well-versed in packaging their job offers with a greater purpose before the larger companies catch up. By following the 3 Rs of Resourcefulness, Resilience, and Right for the company, SMEs can tap into top talent devoted to creating positive impact with the company.

Challenges for Leaders

Although SMEs have a competitive advantage in the talent strategy outlined in this chapter, it does not come without challenges. First, leaders need to have a very clear vision and organizational mission, and this needs to be communicated well to the rest of the company. Many new founders, however, tend to lead business operations organically without a clear vision. The interplay between strategy, technology, and the environment can be very complex in today's market and could derail business executives from developing a vision to strategize with information.[29]

Second, employees could get burnt out from taking on multiple roles in the company, especially when they feel that they are obligated to do so to keep the company running. Leaders need to ensure that well-being and work-life balance are not compromised while providing employees with opportunities to learn new skills. While it is true that employees may have to wear multiple hats in a company due to present constraints, resources still need to be adequately allocated to ensure that workers do not receive excessive workload.

Third, a cohesive culture may be difficult to build at a time of flexible and remote work arrangements. Employees may not have high-quality relationships which can otherwise be built through richer forms of communication and face-to-face interactions. Leaders need to be careful about mandating employees to come back to work physically, as this compromises the aspect of flexibility that many employees value. Adding in the factor of some SMEs having to outsource part of their operations, it might be difficult for offshore employees to truly feel like they are a part of a cohesive team, and companies may need to leverage technological tools to foster bonds with these members as much as possible.

Indeed, according to Chelly, "While these regions (from where we hire remote workers) can offer technically adept candidates at a fraction of the price, successful integration necessitates not only stringent security controls and measures but also fostering a collaborative culture." To overcome this, Responsible Cyber embraces new technological solutions and inclusive strategies. In line with its commitment to building a resilient and diverse workforce that transcends geographical borders, the company has adeptly leveraged Employee of Records (EOR) platforms to streamline its international hiring processes. By utilizing these platforms, Responsible Cyber ensures that it onboards the brightest talents from across the globe, without the complexities often associated with international recruitment. This proactive stance on global talent acquisition not only fortifies its team with a rich tapestry of perspectives and skills but also showcases its dedication to being ahead of the curve.

Despite the disadvantages presented by hiring remote teams, small and medium-sized enterprises can overcome these hurdles with relative ease as there are fewer layers of communication present in the organization. Corrective measures can be taken more quickly and frequent check-ins allow leaders to understand if employees truly feel that they are compatible with the company culture. Adjustments could be made to accommodate to employees' individual needs for meaningful work, while ensuring that the company objectives are met. Using the 3 Rs, SMEs can position themselves strategically as impactful organizations to attract top talent with whom they take on challenges together.

Chapter 7

Leadership

Leadership is undeniably important in bringing organizations forward. In smaller companies with fewer legacy systems and physical resources to keep operations running without human intervention, it is even more important. Research on leadership has been around for about a century, since psychologists studied the theories of individual behavior in the 1900s, understanding human motivation, and identifying the best leadership style that can complement that type of motivation. Yet, this is a never-ending field of research for business and organizational psychologists. Human motivations at the workplace evolve rapidly and what we thought was effective leadership over 100 years ago has now changed.

Before continuing, I would like to make a note at this juncture that there are various topics in leadership not covered in this chapter. Like I mentioned, research on what makes effective leadership can be never-ending. For example, there is much research on the importance of charisma in leadership, but there is debate on whether it can be trained or whether people are simply born with it. There is also research showing that too much charisma is harmful for leader effectiveness. Vergauwe and colleagues found that too little charisma caused leaders to be deemed insufficiently strategic, while high-charisma leaders were rated to be weak on operational behavior (i.e., "all fluff and no result").[1] A moderate level of charisma was important in predicting leadership effectiveness.

There are also scholars who argue that organizations do not need to have a single charismatic individual as a leader if they have a good framework for a vision, with a guiding philosophy instilled not via rhetoric, but through daily action.[2] There is a huge body of literature on crisis leadership, cross-cultural leadership, and even emotionality in leadership.[3,4] In line with the main purpose of this book, the leadership topics discussed in this chapter are attempts at identifying subjects particularly important in smaller companies and particularly relevant in driving future readiness of SMEs. We discuss the four frames of leadership, authentic leadership, and how to lead authentically.

Models of Individual Behavior

One of the earliest forms of effective business leadership is Taylorism, which refers to the system of scientific management popularized by Fred Taylor.[5] It is based on the assumption that factory management is most effective when workers are provided the proper tools and training for their job, and when they are provided with (monetary) incentives for good performance. In "post-Taylor" industries with higher emphasis on creativity, innovation, and knowledge, as opposed to factory-like manufacturing and production, this type of leadership may no longer be effective in motivating workers.

According to the theory of individual behavior, workers evolve from being a rational economic man, to a social man, to a self-actuating man, and now we find ourselves to represent a complex man (Figure 1). A rational economic man[a] is primarily concerned with self-interest and makes decisions based on a rational analysis of potential and desired outcomes. The leadership style most suitable for a rational economic man is transactional leadership, which is a management style based on reward and punishment. It is based on the assumption that employees are extrinsically motivated (i.e., motivated by factors external to the job) to complete work tasks if they are rewarded for them. Consequently, they are also motivated to perform their job if they otherwise receive sanctions or punishment for the inability to do so. Often, rewards include financial incentives such as performance bonuses, with the opposite being pay cuts. It is important to note here that individuals are motivated by

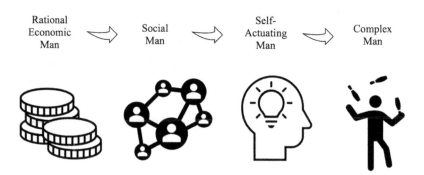

Figure 1. Evolution of models of individual behavior.

---

[a] The word "man" here is used as part of research terminology, but in the context of today's workplace, this refers to individuals of all genders.

rewards (or punishments) upon which they place high *value*. Beyond monetary incentives, rewards could also come in the form of additional days of paid leave, a new title, or public recognition.

Someone who identifies him or herself as primarily a social man is someone who places great importance in relationships and connections with colleagues and superiors at the workplace. Beyond monetary compensation, a social man is dissatisfied at work if they lack meaningful interactions with others at work, as their need for belongingness is not fulfilled. This is not to say that money is not important, but workers may choose to leave an organization that offers "just" money if their social needs are not met.

A self-actuating man is someone who believes that it is important for their talents and potential to be fully realized. Someone with a high need for self-actualization will want to be in a job role that is in line with his or her specialty and passion. The work must provide employees meaning and a sense of purpose, and there must be connection to a grander vision or greater good. While a self-actuating man will typically choose job roles in line with their need for self-actualization, it is increasingly the responsibility of leaders to ensure that employees are in roles they are passionate about. Leaders are also increasingly expected to highlight how individuals' work is related to a more positive impact to society.

To motivate the self-actuating man, one effective way is to display transformational leadership. Unlike transactional leadership which motivates followers using the carrot-and-stick method, transformational leadership places greater focus on inspiring followers, reminding them of a greater purpose that they are working toward. The leader himself or herself exhibits ideal attributes or behaviors and leads by example. Followers are in turn energized to pursue those big goals and are *intrinsically* motivated (i.e., motivated by the job itself) to perform. Examples of transformational leaders are Mahatma Gandhi and Martin Luther King Jr. They galvanized their followers to believe in a vision grander than themselves and to act on that vision, without the need for incentives other than the need to fulfill a higher purpose.

While business leaders are not expected to create social movements like Gandhi and Martin Luther King Jr. did, employees increasingly want managers to exhibit transformational leadership. Characterized by the four "I"s of (i) idealized influence, (ii) inspirational motivation, (iii) intellectual stimulation, and (iv) individual consideration,[6] transformational leaders motivate followers by showing genuine concern for individual employees while encouraging them to take on challenges or stretch goals to develop themselves. As highlighted in Chapter 6, we learnt from the Great Resignation trend that people increasingly choose purpose over job security. We see how human motivations have evolved from over 100 years ago, where human connections start taking a bigger role than money.

Nowadays, we are also increasingly identifying ourselves as the complex man. It is based on the belief that we have multiple needs that should be fulfilled. A complex man wants a financially secure job, social connections, a work with purpose, and also a meaningful life outside of work. Leaders need to provide the complex man with physical, social, and psychological safety. As there is an ongoing war for talent, leaders and companies which can meet these needs the best are in the most advantageous position to recruit the crème de la crème from the talent pool.

Adding another layer of complexity is the fact that human motivations are heterogeneous. Depending on individual personalities and the current stage of their career or life, workers identify themselves in different categories at different points of their lives. In a multi-generational workforce, there are also different groups of employees with categorically different needs. How can leaders fulfill all these needs sufficiently? Will "meeting in the middle" motivate employees equally, or will these efforts from leaders be perceived as half-hearted?

Four Frames of Leadership

To deal with different kinds of challenges at the workplace, Bolman and Deal proposed a four-frame model of leadership. These four frames also take into account a myriad of types of motivation that may be present. These four frames are (i) structural, (ii) human resource (HR), (iii) political, and (iv) symbolic.[7]

Those who lead using the structural frame of leadership view organizations as factories. The world view is one that is based on reason and there is high emphasis on rationality and structure. To solve problems, a structural leader looks at the policies, goals, specialized roles, coordination, and formal relationships, and adjusts these structural elements to encourage performance. The HR leader sees organizations as families. Leaders are seen as servants serving followers and the organization's mission. The focus is on achieving alignment between organizations and individuals, and the leader shows care for members of the organization. For example, Marc Benioff, the CEO of Salesforce, famously pledged no layoffs for 90 days when COVID-19 hit, to allay job security concerns among employees, as the company places the "Ohana", or family culture, of Salesforce at the forefront.

The political frame of leadership involves the fight for limited resources, either as a "warrior" or "peacemaker", and involves skills such as bargaining, negotiation, coercion, compromise, and coalitions around specific interests. Leaders who lead using the political frame identify key players in the organization (blockers, supporters, sponsors, enemies, etc.), understand their stakeholders' interests, map out the political terrain accordingly, and deal with stakeholders based on the amount of power they have in influencing decisions. For a symbolic leader, there is great emphasis on culture and symbols. Leaders appeal to a vision and there is focus on how employees are onboarded, and what the rules, behaviors, and norms in the organization are. Symbolic leaders[b] inspire employees with a sense of purpose and meaning in their work.

The four frames of leadership provide us with useful knowledge on how to deal with different situations. For the same problem, tackling it through different frames could prove to be effective for managers. Let us take the example of an underperforming team member, and let us call him David. Managers could ask the following: What is the root cause of this problem? How is this employee motivated? If David is underperforming because he is not familiar with specific processes, then he should be sent for formalized training (structural). If David was going through a divorce and needed empathy from others while he was going through this temporary difficulty in his life, the HR approach is effective. If David does not budge, but is personally connected to influential decision makers in the organization, the manager might leverage political connections to push David to improve (political). If David is feeling uninspired, the manager could remind him of the significance of his tasks in creating a bigger impact within and outside the organization (symbolic).

---

[b] Symbolic leadership is very similar to transformational leadership. They are not two separate entities — there are merely different lenses through which we analyze leadership (i.e., transactional vs. transformational or four frames of leadership).

A common mistake managers make is placing an underperforming employee on a Personal Improvement Plan (PIP) right away, without understanding the root causes and motivations of this employee. Typically, a PIP not only causes resentment among employees, as they might feel singled out, but also leads to little motivation to change behavior, as employees might perceive that they will be terminated anyway and that the PIP is simply a formality. By truly understanding *why* someone is displaying a certain behavior, equipped with knowledge of the four frames, leaders could deal with day-to-day challenges in the company more effectively.

Utilizing knowledge from the different frames of leadership is especially useful for leaders in SMEs, where there is higher flexibility in how they can solve problems. As in the case of David, an MNC might already have an established system in place, without deeply understanding David's circumstances. In a large organization, following established standard operating procedures (SOPs) is required for efficiency in dealing with a large number of employees. SMEs do not have this limitation. Leaders can afford to take a more personalized approach in dealing with underperforming employees, leading change efforts in the company, getting the company out of a crisis, or even dealing with disgruntled employees who might leave a public bad review. They can afford to tailor leadership styles (while staying authentic) to fit various situations and people.

Crooked Kites Can Fly

To know where leaders' strengths lie in each of the four frames of leadership, there are self-assessments available to identify the styles, or frames, which leaders are naturally inclined to. Connecting these four scores together forms a "Leadership Kite", as shown in Figure 2.

Staying true to ourselves, it is almost impossible to get a perfect diamond shape, where we identify ourselves to be extremely effective in all four frames of leadership. Even globally, many identify themselves to be higher on the structural and HR frames of leadership than the political or symbolic frame. In fact, if one scores 16 out of 24 on the self-assessment for political frame of leadership, one is already in the 90th percentile of all assessment-takers.

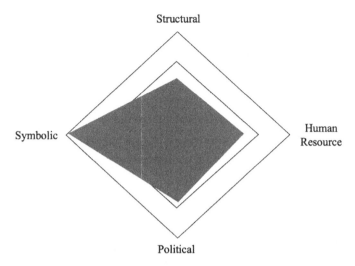

Figure 2. A sample "Leadership Kite" of the four frames of leadership.

If someone scores 16 out of 24 on the structural frame, that individual is only in the 60th percentile of all assessment-takers.[8]

The important thing to remember here is that crooked kites can fly — metaphorically, at least. One can still be an effective leader with low scores on several frames of leadership. Naturally, where there is a weakness, and where situational opportunities allow experimentation and learning, leaders can consciously work on their weaknesses to get a more balanced leadership kite. However, leaning into one's strengths can also prove to very effective, as followers increasingly value authenticity and appreciate a leader for who he or she truly is.

It's Not What You Do, It's Who You Are

Clearly, expectations of what makes an "effective leader" are great. There are already huge expectations of leaders in good times. In crises, leadership is truly put to the test, so much so that stakeholders sometimes expect leaders to act "out of their character" in order to salvage the crisis situation. For example, in high-context cultures, leaders typically gain respect and credibility from followers by showing little to no emotion.[9] However, in times of crises, for example, when it involved the loss of lives as in the COVID-19 pandemic, the missing Malaysia Airlines flight, or the sinking of the Sewol ferry in South Korea, leaders were expected to *display* emotions, especially empathy. Some of the leaders involved in these crises were criticized when they failed to portray emotions or empathy in their public appearances. Yet, if they rose through the ranks based on leadership criteria unrelated to emotions, how can we expect them to "turn on that emotional switch" they were not famed to have?

To be future-ready, leaders need to evolve with the changing needs of their employees, and demands from followers have only been increasing. MBA programs and leadership courses can provide present and future leaders with theoretical knowledge on how to deal with different situations, but how can we accurately define what a future-ready leader is? Is he or she someone who is flexible enough to change their leadership style as and when the situation demands it? Surely this is not possible to expect from one person?

Leadership has evolved tremendously. Traditionally, individuals get promoted to leadership positions due to their technical prowess and when they showcase good performance according to the company's KPIs. Increasingly, collaboration skills are integrated into performance appraisal systems, such that someone is only appraised as a high achiever if he or she demonstrates the ability to work excellently with others. In this traditional model, things like values, ethics, and sustainability merely add an additional layer to leadership.

For example, a leader of a clothing company may start out needing to manage manufacturing operations, plan people, machinery, and materials needed, calculate delivery outputs, and change the clothing style according to fashion trends. In light of sustainability, the leader will additionally need to reconsider materials used, ensure that materials are sustainable (e.g., recycled polyester) and ethically sourced, and review how the company treats their workers (e.g., ensuring that they are paid a living wage). In this example, expert knowledge, managing operations, and managing people remain at the core of leadership, with values and ethics as an additional dimension to leadership.

If one contrasts this to newer expectations of leadership, we see that technical expertise and effective management (in line with Taylorism) are becoming less important in what constitutes the core of leadership. Followers are increasingly looking for someone they look up to and are inspired by. They are convinced by leaders' core values and beliefs, and how they "are" rather than what they "do". Besides, many new technical skills in growing sectors today like AI and sustainability were not in high demand, or did not exist, a decade ago. Having someone in a leadership position because he or she was trained, say, in AI for 20 years, is simply not possible. Yet, leaders are still needed in these companies to drive the organization toward growth in pursuit of future readiness. We increasingly find ourselves needing leaders who are not trained in technical skills, but rather those who display excellent soft skills. They simply "are".

I encourage you to think of the traditional model of leadership like a Christmas tree (Figure 3). At its core, it is a functional tree. At least for a while after its harvest, its leaves remain green, water still flows in its trunk, and it can stand on its own. And then, you layer the tree with decorations — tinsels, ornaments, and the star on top. Finally, you place presents at the bottom of the tree and you are ready to celebrate with the family. Similarly, I would like you to think of the core of leadership — technical knowledge — as the tree. The decorations would be the second layer, which represent skills required in leadership like teamwork, communication, and other functional skills needed to perform the role effectively. Lastly, you have the presents as the final layer, which represent the "being" part of leadership — facets related to values and ethics. If you were to remove these presents, the tree still looks festive enough

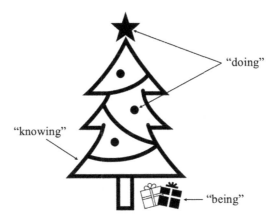

Figure 3. Traditional model of leadership.

Figure 4. Revised model of leadership, with "being" at the core.

for Christmas, and if you were to strip that tree of its tinsels and ornaments, you will still have a functioning tree that is not dependent on the additional layers. In the traditional model of leadership, additional layers can increase leadership effectiveness but are "merely" decorative. These additional layers can even be swapped out. For example, a firm can choose to follow a new sustainability trend, but this is still limited by the amount of technical knowledge present.

Conversely, I would like you to think of the *revised* model of leadership as an ignited flame (Figure 4). Without the inner core that spreads to the middle and outer zones of combustion, we do not have fire at all. In the revised model of leadership, the inner core of the flame represents the "being" — who the leader authentically is, his or her beliefs, and what he or she stands for. The middle zone of the flame represents what the leader does. Again, here, we refer to job-related skills for the functional role to be performed well, which include collaboration and communication. The outer zone represents the technical knowledge held by the leader. Unlike the Christmas tree, the "knowing" and "doing" parts of the flame cannot exist when its core is not there. The flame that we observe stems *from* the "being," while a leader's actions are *driven* by his or her core values. The three layers of leadership in this metaphor act as one entity and no layer can be arbitrarily removed. Strategies and knowledge acquired are based on the values and vision, and not vice versa.

Authentic Leadership

In light of this, authentic leadership comes to the forefront in leading future-ready companies. Authentic leaders lead with vision and values, and encourage authenticity from followers. Authentic leaders are deeply self-aware, display high transparency, have high moral standards, and solicit views of others before making decisions.[10] Results from surveys with 503 executives of SMEs in 2022 and 2023 in collaboration with the World Economic Forum's Self-Assessment Tool for Future Readiness showed that authentic leadership significantly predicts all three pillars of future readiness: long-term growth, societal impact, and adaptive capacity. When findings of this research were presented to business leaders of future-ready SMEs and mid-sized companies in WEF's headquarters in Geneva in December 2022, the concept of authentic leadership also received resounding agreement from participants. Accomplished executives believe that leading with values is the most effective way to attract and retain top talent in today's climate. Staying true to their authentic selves and appealing to a greater vision keep the employees going, especially in difficult times.

Effective leaders also believe that as long as company actions, the organizational culture created, and product offerings are strategically aligned with the company vision, the company should not be afraid of losing employees. As emphasized in Chapter 6, as well as at the beginning of this book, having the "right" fit of employees is paramount for SMEs. Who the company hires, fires, and promotes dictates the way things are handled in the organization. SMEs keen on creating a positive impact on the environment do well if the passion for conserving the environment trickles down from senior leadership to lower-level employees. Hiring practices may need to be modified to allow for this, and more importantly, it requires constant communication from leadership to employees on expected behaviors to support this culture.

Leaders who recognize the importance of authenticity in themselves and in their followers also tend to come to terms with the fact that their organization is not for everyone. A smaller company with fewer resources recognizes that it cannot appeal to the rational economic man, and instead pivots its offering to appeal to the social man or self-actuating man. With the rise of new types of expertise and regular upskilling needed to remain relevant in the market, it also becomes crucial to hire someone not with deep expertise, but with a teachable attitude to adapt to future needs.

Authenticity vs. Ability to Grow

This is not to say that being true to oneself means that individuals are unable to grow. Authenticity remains important in all dealings at the workplace. For example, research has shown that employees value congruence in facial expressions and tone of feedback. If leaders delivered negative feedback with positive facial affect, they were perceived as inauthentic and received less favorable leader ratings.[11] Yet, leaders who lack emotional intelligence and the ability to regulate their emotions cannot continue to lead in a way that negatively impacts others around them and claim that they are being authentic. Bosses who react to situations explosively and with "hot" negative emotions should understand that authenticity does not equate with the inability to grow.

While "true-to-selfers" are perceived as more authentic, they may need to evolve their style as they gain insight and experience over time.[12] In the instance of the explosive leader, it is important for the leader to develop emotional awareness of himself or herself, as well as emotional awareness of others around them. The leader could engage in mindfulness practices such as meditating, ensuring that there is a pause before responding to a situation, and being fully present in interactions with team members, where the leader observes without judgment.[13] In providing negative feedback, instead of faking emotional expression during the process, leaders should integrate aspects of effective leadership highlighted previously. Transformational leaders who are genuinely concerned about individuals' professional development can frame the negative feedback as an opportunity for improvement, while allowing the employee space to feel disheartened by the negative news.

Perpetuating negative behaviors in the name of "authenticity" is not the goal. Besides, we observe how top talent leaves workplaces which are "toxic" in pursuit of an organizational culture that treats them with more respect.[14] It is important for leaders to continue striving for self-improvement while being aware of their strengths and limitations. For instance, with reference to the four frames of leadership by Bolman and Deal, new leaders might be naïve to believe that they are high on all four frames of leadership and can lead any and

every situation effectively. In reality, they might only be efficient in two of the four frames, and may feel uncomfortable using the other two frames to manage their team. Authenticity involves a willingness to learn and being comfortable with the uncomfortable growth process. Authenticity is an end goal, not the starting point.

How to Lead Authentically

I often hear from my MBA students that circumstances make it very difficult for them to lead authentically. Especially if one is in a mid-management position with multiple stakeholders to be accountable to, being completely honest might backfire. For example, if a new leader enters a company and openly admits that he or she does not know much about the operations and wishes to learn from the team, this new leader will not gain much credibility. This could negatively affect future interactions, from which the leader might not recover. While it is important to not be dishonest (i.e., one should not say he or she is capable of something when they are not), authentic selves should be portrayed appropriately. For instance, in a crisis situation, it makes most sense to shield employees from the full extent of the problems behind the scenes. This is to keep emotions from running high as the team needs to be in the correct mindset to re-strategize and move forward.

Also, authentic leadership relies heavily on positive relationships between leaders and followers, and this type of trust and high-quality relationships cannot be cultivated overnight. Before being able to lead with authenticity, much work needs to be invested in self-development, creating a "story", and truly understanding one's core values. To start the journey, the following are some practical recommendations.

Identify Core Values

Self-awareness is a very crucial part of leadership. In the survey with 503 leaders of SMEs, out of the four dimensions of authentic leadership, self-awareness was the only dimension that consistently predicted all three dimensions of future readiness positively. In other words, while authentic leadership is a higher-order construct comprising four dimensions, self-awareness could "stand on its own" in predicting a company's level of future readiness. To increase one's

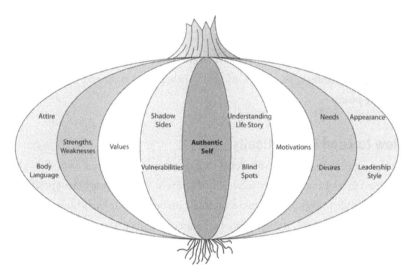

Figure 5. Onion exercise to identify core values.[15]

self-awareness, leaders could engage in exercises to identify their core values, strengths, and passion.

One such exercise is what we call the "onion exercise" (Figure 5). Much like peeling layers of an onion to find its core, we peel superficial layers of ourselves to understand what truly drives us. An example of the onion exercise is listing out incidents in one's past experiences that caused the most anger as well as incidents that ignited the most passion. The idea is that when one cross-references these two lists, there will appear a unifying theme that represents a core value.

I ran this exercise with about 80 MBA students in a course called Leading with Impact. One of my students gave the following example: He is most angry when circumstances drive him to have to break trust in relationships. In this instance, his superior told him that the company had to reject services from a particular vendor, with whom he had built trusting relationships. Having to "betray" this business partner did not sit well with him. Conversely, he is most happy when users are satisfied with the company's product. He is passionate about helping others and it brings him joy if he is able to contribute to user satisfaction. Here, we identified the unifying theme as *people*. Building and maintaining meaningful relationships with others is extremely important to him. Leading authentically in his view involves heavy emphasis on connections and well-being.

With the same exercise, we identified that for some others, core values revolved around justice, a sense of control, and self-development. We then identified leadership styles that match these values. Where people represent a core value, one could lean into the HR frame of leadership. For sense of control, one could use the structural frame of leadership to design systems to ensure that things are operated in a way where outcomes are predictable. Where the core value revolves around self-development, complementary leadership involves including challenges at work and understanding the importance of self-actualization.

Being completely honest with this exercise requires a degree of vulnerability and being okay with being "exposed". It might appear easy to "just be oneself", but with the various expectations from employees, shareholders, consumers, board members, and society in general, company leaders could find this exercise difficult as their core value might run contrary to stakeholder expectations. For instance, a leader passionate about furthering the professional development of his or her people might receive pushback from stakeholders when it comes to how they budget staff training versus investment in, say, digital infrastructure. Balancing needs and expectations from various stakeholders while leading according to one's version of his or her authentic self requires virtues not taught in traditional classes.

Write (and Rewrite) Your "Story"

We often have a couple of defining stories from our childhood or early in our careers that define who we are as leaders. Many, if not all, of the entrepreneurs whom I interviewed knew exactly the defining moment when they decided to start their company. They were very clear about the problem in the market or society which they wanted to solve, and this story gets repeated over and over in their internal and external communications. The stories ranged from "When I started working in company XYZ, I was bitten by the entrepreneur bug and that was also where I met my mentor in my founder journey" to "I met these smart people from the ABC community and I thought we had to do something to give them opportunities" to "They lost my passport, I missed my flight, and I had to stay in the country longer. That gave me an opportunity to spend time with the community there and that is what inspired my entrepreneur journey". Whether the path to leadership was planned or serendipitous, the authentic leaders I encountered always had a defining personal story.

What MBA programs and leadership courses often lack is this ability to give up-and-coming leaders a *story*. How many of us have our defining story in our back pockets? How many of us are even aware of our core values? Are we ready to peel superficial layers of ourselves to come to the core of the "onion", and are we courageous enough to lead according to that core? To start leading authentically, the journey to increased self-awareness could thus begin with various self-assessments and exercises to first understand one's core value(s) and to leverage these values to pick a personal story that defines who an individual is as a leader.

That being said, a self-aware leader should understand that as one gains more insights and experiences in the leadership journey, one's "story" can also change. Changing one's story does not mean that he or she is being inauthentic. Granted, one should not change stories too often, and presenting different stories to different stakeholders could lead to perceptions of inauthenticity if the leader is seen as a "chameleon". However, it actually alludes to *greater* self-awareness if a leader realizes that lessons gleaned from life experiences allow him or her to expand the definition of an authentic leader.

For me as an educator, my defining narrative has always been one that revolved around my parents and my upbringing. Growing up with four other siblings, a mother who was a housewife, and a father who had to work two jobs to financially support the family, it was ingrained in me that *education* was one way for us to move upward in social mobility. My mother told me that in order to do well in life, I must do well in school. I was dependent on government bursaries, and without a full scholarship to university, my family would have had a hard time supporting my studies. I often tell this story to others as to why I wanted to be an educator and a leader of young minds, in that I truly believe that education is a tool for upward social mobility as it was for me.

Just over a year ago, my mother passed away rather suddenly. Yes, this grief was personal, but what I realized from this is that my motivations to be an educator became even stronger. I reflected upon what my mother left behind

and what stood out were not material possessions or inheritance. What she left behind were the lessons and *values* that she imbued in me, and *they* will never die. That redefined my purpose as an educator. It was no longer just about conveying theories and concepts for business management. It became about passing on values that will positively impact my students' lives and enable them to be the best versions of themselves. My defining story still centered on my parents, but one revolved around life, and the other around death.

Journey to Authenticity through Growing Pains

Sometimes, "growing pains" are just that. We go through difficult times and come out the other end with battle scars, but stronger for it, i.e., we grow through the pain. For founders of small and medium-sized enterprises, one can multiply these difficult times by 100, 1,000, or according to the CEO of Nvidia, Jensen Huang, even a million.[16] In pursuing self-development, one might find himself or herself having to let go of outdated values and one might feel "fake" in the process. Didn't the leader champion initiative X in the past to improve the organizational structure? Why is the company now restructuring yet again?

It is okay to evolve. In fact, it is good to evolve. A leader who restructured the organization to improve operational efficiency might now put ethics and governance at the forefront, and restructuring the company again to reflect the integration of governance in the business model becomes important. This not only reflects the evolution of the CEO as a leader but also keeps the business future-ready as the company's values are updated and are now better aligned with society. Learning to learn is indispensable, and leaders and company cultures that allow for this across the different levels of the organization come out on top.

Part Five

Change Management

Chapter 8
Just Pivot

In the previous chapters of this book, the roles of different organizational elements in increasing companies' future readiness levels were highlighted. For SMEs to pursue one or several of these strategies, they will need to engage in change management. But, how are SMEs capable of thinking of change, when they find themselves in constant firefighting mode, solving pressing problems on a daily basis, or without sufficient cash reserves to experiment with innovative ideas? Throughout the book, I have featured various companies from different industries and regions, and highlighted how they embody future readiness at different stages of organizational development. For some, a future-ready business model and vision were present at the inception of the company. For others, it involved a pivot, with an understanding that for an organization to remain resilient, it may need to change its value proposition.

Overcoming inertia is an uphill battle for any company; for a small firm with few resources, it might seem almost impossible. My hope for this book is to get founders and business leaders of SMEs to realize that they currently find themselves at the *best* possible position for change. In a VUCA world with rapid change, large companies, despite their wealth in resources, find it difficult to mobilize multiple stakeholders to make adaptations to the changing needs of the market. Our current market environment favors actors who are nimble, agile, and willing to learn. To remain competitive, learning must accelerate faster than the pace of change. Small and medium-sized enterprises with an agile mindset stand to reap the most benefit from the global situation.

In this chapter, we will go through classic and contemporary theories on change management, highlight the biggest barriers to change, and provide SMEs with several possible strategies to overcome these barriers to pursue future readiness.

Reactive vs. Proactive Change

There are three routes to innovation. The traditional route involves product development as a response to the current market environment. This often includes conducting market research, assessing customer needs, making incremental changes to the current product, and then launching it to market. The second route is more ambidextrous. It is structured, but agile innovation. It involves exploration — trying out unfamiliar choices and new approaches — on the one hand and exploitation — sticking to the current business model for stable value creation — on the other hand. The third route is when innovation becomes part and parcel in the way the organization works. Project sprints become a scalable, repeatable, and standardized operating procedure in the company. The focus is less on whether an idea is executed or not but more on the fact that ideas regularly go through the innovation process of ideating, operationalizing, and evaluating. In this process, the organizational elements we discussed throughout this book, like autonomy, psychological safety, and encouraging risk-taking and failure, are important.

These three routes show a progression from a reactive stance to change to a proactive one. Plagued with a myriad of immediate concerns, SMEs might find themselves being more reactionary to change as opposed to proactively making changes to their environment. Again, a common theme throughout this book is to highlight that the biggest disruptors of the industry are usually small and medium-sized companies. There are fewer legacy models they have to hold on to and fewer stakeholders to get buy-in from. Besides, SMEs tend to be disadvantaged in the traditional product development route due to fewer resources invested in R&D compared to their larger counterparts. Indeed, incorporating a multi-faceted innovation framework in a company's operations is what SMEs should aspire toward.

Disruption Does Not Have to be Costly

Coined in the early 1990s by the late Harvard Business School professor Clayton Christensen, disruptive innovation refers to a process by which a product or service takes root in simple applications at the bottom of a market, and eventually displaces established competitors as it is a dramatically cheaper and simpler innovation that attracts new users and creates new markets.[1]

Disruptive innovation does not necessarily require a big, radical, expensive change. Indeed, according to directors of Bain & Company, Darrell Rigby and Alistair Corbett, disruptive innovation should not cost a fortune.[2] The idea is for a disruptive project to generate wins or profits quickly, as early wins open the way for larger projects to target larger markets. Keeping disruption development as simple as possible, with "few bells, no whistles" as Rigby and Corbett put it, together with lower investment per project, allows the company to pursue more disruptive innovations without diluting earnings. In fact, the authors recognized start-ups and smaller companies as being more associated with disruptive innovations than established ones.

It is important to understand here that disruptive innovation is a strategy, not a technology. We have discussed previously that technology can indeed be used as a conduit to enact positive change, but the company's *vision* to impact society positively can and should be detached from technology. In the example of Kuza, the Kenyan-based micro-learning platform for farmers, technology is indeed used to empower its users, but the vision of helping the "bottom billion" is independent of technology and its apps. Kuza would have found different ways to reach this vision if the technological field looked different.

Guided on whether innovations achieve strategic alignment with a company's vision, disruptive innovation does not have to be expensive. Netflix famously started out by introducing its monthly DVD subscription service in 1997 for the low price of US$8.99/month, allowing customers to rent an unlimited number of DVDs. By 2002, it was mailing about 190,000 discs a month to its more than 670,000 subscribers. In 2007, as bandwidth costs and data speeds were improving significantly, Netflix then introduced its online streaming service, available on almost any device with an Internet connection.[3] In the meantime, Blockbuster, the main player in the entertainment industry, continued its traditional business model. Netflix overtook Blockbuster, and Blockbuster eventually filed for bankruptcy in 2010.

Classic Model of Organizational Decline

The case of Blockbuster was typical of what we observe in a model of organizational decline. This model was developed by William Weitzel and Ellen Jonsson in 1989 and consists of five stages.[4] Under the assumption of rationality, organizations attempt to anticipate and adapt to environmental changes, failure of which will ultimately lead to the company decline.[5] In the first stage of organizational decline, the Blinded stage, the firm is not aware of the changes in the environment and of the steps it needs to take to adapt to these changes. Blockbuster was not paying attention to the introduction and expansion of Netflix. A company in the Blinded stage is unable to match disruption strategies with the disruption sensitivities, as it fails to scan, analyze, and monitor for potential threats to the business.

In the second stage, Inaction, the company fails to act on these potential threats in the environment. The third stage, Faulty Action, is when the company realizes that action needs to be taken, but engages in the wrong decisions, which leads to the fourth stage, Crisis. Without a radical change to turn things around and save the company, the organization ultimately reaches the last stage, Dissolution.

Inaction or Faulty Action?

Eastman Kodak Co. has been touted as an example of a company that paid the price of Inaction. During the rise of digital photography, Kodak failed to innovate in time to keep up with its competitors. Many accounts of the events portrayed Kodak as ignoring and failing to embrace new technology. However, the reality was that Kodak built the first digital camera in 1975. In the 1990s, senior leaders were "acutely aware" of the emerging trend of digital photography, but technological and management difficulties prevented Kodak from shifting from analog to digital photography.[6]

First, digital imaging was based on a general-purpose semiconductor technology platform, and this had nothing to do with the process of manufacturing film. Competing in this different technological space brought tremendous challenges. Second, internal strife was present in the company as it was a "complicated and emotional" issue to deal with the thousands of people in the legacy businesses that were destined to shrink.[7] Kodak was mainly preoccupied with preserving its current business model that had declining profit margins, while legacy costs remained high.

Looking back, Kodak could have attempted to compete on capabilities rather than on the markets that it was in.[8] It could have redirected its skills in complex organic chemistry and high-speed coating toward other products involving complex materials, as Fuji did. It could also have proactively exited its legacy businesses in a timely way like IBM Corp. Between the early 1990s and the 2000s, IBM exited markets which included printer manufacturing, flat panel displays, personal computers, and disk drives, thereby reducing costs. Kodak could have used the opportunity to restructure — which it eventually did with its consumer film business, now owned by Kodak's UK pension plan.

The greatest barriers to innovations are often organizational ones. SMEs are in a better position than giants like Kodak to escape the traps of inaction and faulty action.

Microsoft almost fell into this situation. In 1994, its rival Netscape introduced a better way to surf the World Wide Web and Microsoft almost let the Internet pass it by. Bill Gates dismissed the Internet as being too hard to use, calling the browser "trivial".[9] Meanwhile, Netscape's market share rose to almost 90 percent, while Microsoft's stock prices decreased. It was then that Gates decided to make probably "the biggest U-turn in the history of Microsoft", circulating a memo among senior staff titled "Internet Tidal Wave". This memo recognized the improved communication technology and the expanded access to the Internet, as well as outlining Microsoft's new strategy of placing the Internet at the forefront of its future developments. The Internet was "assigned the highest level of importance" and Microsoft engineers were to focus their energies solely on products with the Internet at their core.[10]

Gates managed to avert crisis and turned Microsoft around by reallocating the company's resources and reprioritizing its strategies. A large company like Microsoft may have sufficient slack resources to buffer losses from its initial misstep, but smaller companies may not. Where SMEs have the advantage, however, is in the ability to re-strategize quicker than a big company like Microsoft. It is easier to dismantle current methods of working, get employees on board with new changes, and reestablish new approaches.

To be future-ready, it is important for companies to avoid the Blinded stage in the first place. SMEs should scan the big external factors in the environment that can let in big disruptors. The main factors, as highlighted earlier in the book, are linked to technology and sustainability.

Don't Overinvest in Technology

I might sound like a broken record here, but I am stressing again that technology should be seen as a *means* to grow and expand into new markets, and is not the be-all and end-all. While it is important to look out for trends and make sure not to miss them, many companies make the mistake of making the technology too elegant and overinvesting in innovation. This may mean that the company enters the market with its innovation too little too late, while its competitors have already clinched their respective segments of the market.

What is important is to be cognizant of the *organizational vision* and the environmental and societal *impact* that the company wants to create. For example, while AI has many potential benefits, companies need not hop on to the AI train if there is no strategic alignment with the company's business model. In the legal system, for instance, AI may be used to proofread depositions and legal documents, but given its potential to exacerbate biases, it should not be involved in verdicts and sentencing. In companies, AI Chatbots may help customers resolve routine enquiries and reduce queue times. Yet, various reports show that more than 80% of consumers still prefer dealing with human beings for customer service.[11,12] In a 2022 study, while AI Chatbots performed better than human customer service professionals when the product attribute was functional, humans outperformed AI when the product attribute was experiential.[13] If stellar customer service with the human touch represents the crux of a company's value proposition and vision, this should not be outsourced to AI.

Design Thinking: Empathy

Instead of turning to the latest technological trends to create additional value, disruptive innovation comes from *truly* understanding customers' needs and reimagining a product, service, or process to address these needs. Here, I refer to one of the core tenets of Design Thinking — empathy. Design Thinking entails a human-centered approach to innovation.[14] Grounded in the three "I"s of Inspiration, Ideation, and Implementation, Design Thinking goes to the core of the issue and the resulting solution from this process may be truly revolutionary.

In the Inspiration phase, thorough research is conducted on the business problems, opportunities, observing what others in the market do, and assessing the constraints that the company has (e.g., time, lack of resources, shrinking market). This also involves going to the customers and asking them about their needs, behaviors, and possibly sources of negative emotions related to the product or service. Then, information is organized and synthesized such that it tells different stories; the more stories, the better.

At the Ideation phase, brainstorming occurs. Ideas are generated, prototypes (and revisions to the prototypes) are built, tested, and retested, and stories from earlier are kept alive. The Implementation phase involves engineering the product, service, or experience, and making a use case. Design Thinking challenges members of the organization to go under the surface to come up with a solution that may not be thought of through the conventional product development route. A simple yet disruptive innovation can arise from this.

An example comes in the form of the Breast Service Project, a project conducted in two hospitals in New Zealand to improve the healthcare of breast cancer patients. Using a six-step process of Design Thinking (engage, plan, explore, develop, decide, and change), researchers found that patients experienced high levels of anxiety not when they learnt that they have breast cancer, but rather during the waiting times for mammography, biopsy, and clinical appointments.[15] This was especially the case when staff was uninformative or impolite. As anxiety and negative emotions have been linked to poor recovery, it is crucial to adopt a patient-centered approach to healthcare.

The issue faced by patients was less about the medical procedures that they would have to go through should they have breast cancer and more about the fact that they were kept in the dark about the results, which resulted in higher anxiety. The solutions then revolved around quicker communication with the patients and their families, encouraging staff to display kindness and empathy toward patients, and providing one constant point of contact so that patients could have one reliable staff member for treatment-related information. This intervention tackled patient *experience* to improve healthcare, as opposed to investing more in treatment options, medical devices, or hospital equipment.

Similarly, SMEs can benefit from adopting an open-minded, holistic approach to solving problems. Led by empathy, low-cost solutions can enact positive change. Clearly, future-ready SMEs will need to adopt a proactive stance to change. They need to anticipate trends to avoid finding themselves in the Blinded stage of organizational decline, and encouraging an empathy-led process to design solutions is beneficial, though it may require additional buy-in from other members of the company. For companies finding themselves in a state of organizational inertia and finding it impossible to change, I propose resolving this through a revised understanding of urgency.

Revised Understanding of Urgency

John Kotter, Emeritus professor at Harvard Business School, popularized an 8-step change management model which is used in many MBA courses on Change Management.[16] The first step involves creating a sense of urgency, as members of the organization need to understand that change is essential to overcome inertia. The next steps involve (2) forming a powerful guiding coalition, (3) creating a vision, (4) communicating that new vision, (5) empowering employees to act on that vision and removing blockers, (6) recognizing and rewarding changed behaviors in the short term, (7) consolidating changes, which could involve hiring, promoting, and developing employees who can implement the vision, as well as by appointing change agents, and (8) institutionalizing new approaches, where there is an organization-wide understanding that the changed behaviors and systems are linked to corporate success.

To even reach the first step of the change management model, there needs to be a revised understanding of urgency. For decision makers in SMEs, "urgent problems" often include decisions related to the company's immediate survival, such as funding and capital, as well as filling roles with the right talent. Things like sustainability and digital innovation often take a back seat as founders' top concerns. However, the reality is that sustainability and technology issues

are urgent. In Chapter 4, I highlighted how the carbon tax rate will increase nine-fold within the next five years and 16 times its current rate in six years. If companies do not start rethinking about their greenhouse gas (GHG) emissions now, the exorbitant costs incurred in the next few years will reduce their competitiveness in the market. Cybersecurity is also a pressing issue and companies are at risk of losing valuable data and spending precious resources recovering from cyberattacks if they do not increase their data readiness levels.

A revised understanding of urgency helps SMEs embark on their transformation journey. Elon Musk famously founded SpaceX because he believes that it is imperative to go to space to save Earth.[17] Similarly, when leaders realize that digital innovation, understanding AI, and incorporating ESG into the business model are not merely "nice-to-have" features to lend them a competitive advantage, but rather are *imperative* for them to survive in the future, change management can start.

Unfreeze, Change, Refreeze

Another model of change management that is used by organizations was developed by Kurt Lewin in the 1940s.[18] The model considers change as a process with three distinct stages. The Unfreeze stage involves challenging the *status quo*, spreading awareness that the existing structure, systems, and processes no longer serve the purpose of the organization. Not only do structural elements of the organization need to change but the behaviors, attitudes, and skills of the workforce also require a shift. The Change phase is when these revisions to the systems and the workforce are implemented. The Refreeze phase, much like the last step of Kotter's change management model, involves institutionalizing changes through modifications in the organizational culture and reward system, such that the new way of working is normalized and internalized through the company's daily operations.

Again, this is a huge feat for larger corporations. Louis Gerstner, former CEO of IBM, even likened the company to an elephant when he was leading IBM through dramatic change, highlighting how difficult it was to get an elephant to "dance".[19] "Melting", implementing, and later "solidifying" changes are easier in smaller companies because there are fewer barriers to change, less resistance from employees, and more cohesion from organizational members to work toward a new vision together.

Barriers to Change

The examples in this chapter illustrate two main barriers to change: (i) legacy business models and (ii) people. It is difficult to move away from a successful business formula with a known track record for value creation. Also, a large proportion of all SMEs are family-owned businesses. In Spain, 70% of Spanish SMEs are family businesses,[20] in the UK, the percentages hover between 74% and 89%,[21] and 85% of the companies in the Asia Pacific region are owned by a family group.[22] Although not all SMEs are family-owned and vice versa, the emotional ties to an original business model, together with leadership succession challenges, can mean that change is complicated for a large segment of SMEs.

As goals and values of family members evolve and become more diverse, differences in opinions on how to lead, grow, or change the direction of a company can cause conflict, making change management in these companies tricky. Besides, next-generation leaders could lack the necessary skills to take over the business — if they wish to run the business at all — as the older generation may cling on to control.

This leads us to the second barrier to change: people. Resistance to change is natural. Humans experience what we call the *status quo* bias — a preference for maintaining one's current situation — which is so ingrained in us that it forms part of what is termed System 1 thinking. System 1 thinking is a quick, automatic, emotional response to information that we are confronted with. We evolved to have these biases and System 1 thinking because it benefits us. We cannot possibly slowly and systematically analyze all pieces of information that we receive, and given that we make approximately 35,000 decisions per day,[23] relying on our cognitive biases saves us time and effort, and allows us to function in our roles without being overwhelmed.

In organizational change, the stakes go beyond our natural inclination toward *status quo* bias. Real jobs may be deemed obsolete, livelihoods may be affected, and family members dependent on employees' incomes may have

their lives upended. So, how do we overcome these barriers? The concerns are real and the consequences are large.

Overcoming Barriers to Change: Lean In

We have repeatedly highlighted that it is easier for smaller companies to overcome barriers to change. Fewer levels of hierarchy and less established protocols mean that organizational processes are more fluid and thus more susceptible to change, a change in vision can be more easily communicated to the fewer stakeholders in SMEs compared to large corporations, and a loyal workforce — as highlighted in Chapter 6 — catalyzes a unified move in a new direction for the company. It is easier to rally support for change, not only because of the smaller number of employees but also because of the higher alignment of values between the organization, leaders, and employees. However, the barriers highlighted could prove to be tricky due to the emotional, and not structural, nature of these factors.

To overcome family conflicts that may arise out of organizational change, experts suggest engaging external parties for mediation.[24] In this manner, emotions may be removed from the situation, as all parties are encouraged to adopt an objective, rational stance — otherwise known as System 2 thinking — which involves more deliberate and effortful thoughts in making decisions. Structural changes can also be implemented, such as providing the next generation of leaders opportunities to gain global experience in relevant ecosystems, like banking, private equity, accounting, management consulting, or entrepreneurship, before joining the family business officially.[25]

Beyond complementing the System 1 way of thinking with System 2 solutions, I would even suggest *leaning into* the emotional nature of these barriers to change. According to a Family Business Survey conducted by Price waterhouse Coopers in 2021, when asked to name their top priorities for the next two years, family businesses in the Asia Pacific listed expansion and/or diversification (82%) as their top priority.[26] This was followed by digital, innovation, and technology (77%) and improving or evolving new thinking (66%). These priorities are very much in line with concerns of SMEs as per the global study conducted between 2021 and 2023 with the World Economic

Forum. In this vein, I appeal to these companies' emotional interest in keeping control of their business in that it is *only through change* that their *company's legacy can be safeguarded*. Having existed for so long and having experienced multiple turbulences and shocks only make the organization more resilient. To continue being resilient, one must embrace change to secure the company's future.

Similarly, emotional appeals can be made to encourage employees to overcome their initial resistance to change. First, senior leadership must not only explain the "What" of organizational change but also the "Why". More importantly, communication must be tailored to various stakeholders of the company. What is in it for them? How do shareholders benefit from a pivot to ESG? How will employees' workload be reduced through automation? And, how can they use this additional time to upskill?

Second, members of the organization can be empowered to enact change. The company can appoint change agents who champion these new initiatives internally and externally. Not only does this increased autonomy for employees get them to be more committed to the cause and the organization, closer relationships among employees in smaller companies also mean that these change agents can leverage their emotional ties to convince others be on board. Here, empathy again comes to the forefront, as members seek to understand the underlying reasons behind resistance to change and address them specifically.

Mindset Change: Leadership and People as an Asset

For a company to be agile, innovation scholar Stephen Denning argued that it primarily involves a mindset shift.[27] Agile management requires strong inspirational leadership, where managers see themselves as enablers rather than controllers. To be agile at scale, companies need to form agile teams, which are made up of representatives from different departments of the company, i.e., cross-functional teams. Agile teams are project-oriented, and as highlighted earlier in this chapter, run projects in sprints to achieve set objectives. By "compressing" the organizational structure, agile teams gather information from different departments and through cyclical and iterative stages, deliver early in the lifecycle to generate value as quickly as possible.

While "agile at scale" may be more relevant to medium-sized enterprises than small companies, what is important to recognize here is that we cannot assume that adding more agile teams in business processes automatically makes the organization more agile. It requires embodying the spirit of continuous improvement, from leadership to followers. People are truly an asset in SMEs, and the quicker the acceptance or acquisition of this agile mindset in organizations, the easier it is for SMEs to "just pivot".

Case Study: PALO IT

"We fail fast, and we fail forward." The CEO of PALO IT, Stanislas Bocquet, strongly believes that failing, taking calculated risks, and empowering employees help propel innovations that contribute to the company's success.

PALO IT is a global innovation and software development company dedicated to helping organizations craft tech as a force for good. It works with clients to rapidly launch products and services, create new business models, and prepare leadership and culture for the future. Using methods like Design Thinking, Agile, and DevOps, PALO IT helps businesses and governmental agencies enact digital transformation through web and app development, software design, and project management.

With B Corp certification in its offices in Singapore, Hong Kong, Thailand, and Mexico, and led by the company motto "Crafting Tech as a Force for Good", PALO IT is committed to using technology to create sustainable solutions. Further to that, the company has been a member of the WEF New Champions program since 2021, of which CEO Stanislas Bocquet is currently a board member.

PALO IT has worked with many renowned clients such as BNP Paribas, Allianz, BMW, and VISA. The Singapore office also worked closely with the Government Technology Office to accelerate the production of TraceTogether, a digital system that facilitated contact tracing efforts in response to the COVID-19 pandemic in Singapore. Sustainability and societal good are at the forefront of PALO IT's business operations. Recently, in June 2023, it also partnered with Climate Impact X (CIX), a Singapore-based marketplace and exchange for trusted carbon credits, to launch CIX's spot exchange trading platform.[28] By increasing access and connectivity to global carbon markets, PALO IT plays a crucial role in the launch of the CIX Exchange in a bid to reduce emissions.

Vision Pivot in PALO IT

However, pursuing green growth opportunities was not always on the business agenda for PALO IT. Even though Bocquet founded the company in 2009, he had a revelation in 2015. Bocquet said, "In 2015, I realized that sustainability was talked about more and more by businesses and leaders. When I spoke about this strategy to my friends and clients, most of them were skeptical." Yet, Bocquet persisted with this idea and consulted his team. Bocquet decided on a bottom-up approach to creating a new vision for the company.

"We decided to experiment, a new approach: appreciative inquiry. We asked our employees around the world — we had about 200 employees at that time — to gather at a retreat in Phuket, Thailand. For four days, we had intense workshops and we asked everyone to share one thing: 'What is your personal dream?' Then, we used those personal dreams to transform the direction of the company," mentioned Bocquet. Such empowerment of the employees is a quintessential part of the organizational culture present in PALO IT. "We realize that our people are our solution builders and innovators. All the employees could own part of the responsibility in transforming the company. We understand their strengths, and they came up with some crazy ideas for transformation. We read them together." Indeed, from those "crazy ideas", PALO IT made significant changes to the company.

First, it pivoted its vision to focus on the UN's Sustainable Development Goals. While the company has executed many projects in the past with a focus on societal impact, PALO IT decided to exclusively use "tech for good". This meant ensuring that the values of the clients are aligned to those of the company and being prepared to give up on several business opportunities. "When we start the first conversation [with a customer], it's 'super natural' because we have the same vision and the same core values. But also, you have to accept that you are going to lose part of your business [if they do not align]." Despite having to turn down potential work, PALO IT continues to grow as new customers want to work with the company precisely due to its impact-focused vision, as well as through recommendations from existing clients.

Second, the management structure was changed to increase autonomy and knowledge-sharing. "We changed the committee because at the beginning, it was more of the management team who was driving the company. However, from 2015 onward, in our respective country offices, everybody is empowered to be part of the adventure." Reaching a 90% rate of happy employees, especially when tech companies typically report high levels of employee burnout, is a testament to the positive organizational climate provided at PALO IT. "We have communities of experts within the company. They do their job, but they will also improve their work in their own way, with a strategic vision. We also have communities of people with the same interest, let's say blockchain, who spend time together and share knowledge [on the topic]," added Bocquet.

Third, PALO IT started measuring its impact. It aims to be a net-zero company by 2025, have more than 50% of revenue from projects with a positive impact, train 100% of its employees on impact, and target all 18 of its offices to attain B Corp Certification. While the leadership team regularly analyzes different trends and examines how they are relevant to the company's path for the future, it is also committed to reassessing the vision and core values of the organization every 6 months to ensure that the company operates in a way that continues to care about the planet.

Size and Company Culture as Advantages for Pivot

Even though PALO IT has grown to over 700 employees at the moment, this pivot to a new direction for the company was made more possible due to its size at the time. As a medium-sized enterprise, PALO IT is a prime example of how a company can take advantage of an upcoming market opportunity and, together with a cohesive and dedicated workforce, prove its naysayers wrong and embark on a transformation journey to improve its position in the tech consultancy market.

SMEs vs. MNCs

We observe from the case study of PALO IT that change management in SMEs can take a very different form than in MNCs. In SMEs, a bottom-up approach of changing a company's vision is very much possible, provided that the right culture and mindset are in place. Lower-level employees' opinions are heard and integrated in changes in the company. In MNCs, taking some of Gerstner's principles to turn IBM around, organizational change is often led by senior leadership. While big companies also utilize Design Thinking and innovate customer-centric products, they often make structural changes to motivate change behavior *extrinsically*, as opposed to smaller companies' heavier reliance on employees' loyalty and *intrinsic* motivation to change and grow. In the example of IBM, when Gerstner noticed that there was a culture of jealousy and people trying to overpower each other, the reward system in the company was revamped to focus on total corporate performance instead of individual units.[29]

Similarly, the impetus for change may be different in SMEs compared to MNCs. SMEs may want to change the direction of the company due to necessity, e.g., keeping up with their competitors, while MNCs have more resources to make a strategic change to capture a larger share of the market. Yet, SMEs are in a more advantageous position to make a proactive, rather than reactive, change. Indeed, Gerstner encouraged IBM to "operate as an entrepreneurial organization", recognizing that small companies are most nimble to adapt to changes. Embracing the Agile mindset, together with a revised understanding of urgency, can nudge SMEs to feel empowered to make active changes to become future-ready.

Foresight Planning

Foresight planning is the new way of management. As highlighted in the introduction of this book, one thing that we can predict about the future is that it is unpredictable. Foresight planning embraces and recognizes that the future is more fragile than before and involves focusing on the long term by analyzing situations from multiple perspectives. It is essentially a lens through which organizations can understand how issues unfolding today can impact them in the future.

Two well-known methods used in foresight are horizon scanning and scenario planning. Horizon scanning involves examining elements that are present in megatrends, trends, weak signals (e.g., first symptoms of climate change like the rising ocean levels), wildcards (low-probability events like 9/11), and even uncertainties (e.g., long-term impact of AI) and incorporating these elements in business strategies. Companies can then categorize them into "no-brainers" (short-term impactful trends which should be incorporated immediately), "alarms" (trends which might be impactful and require further research), and "parking" (trends with very low impact on the industry).[30] Scenario planning involves simulations of possible futures. While these do not represent actual predictions, engaging in scenario planning helps project decision makers in an unpredictable future environment, from where they can formulate potential responses or educate relevant stakeholders.

Foresight is increasingly perceived as a key strategic ability which requires futures thinking (the ability to explore and perceive alternative futures), systems thinking (the ability to understand the bigger picture from analyzing different factors in the environment), and exponential thinking (the ability to understand that something small today could have a huge impact very quickly). It requires embracing peripheral and systemic views, and it does not involve answering questions right, but asking the right questions. What are some possible futures that may play out for us in the next five years? What are some possible futures that may not? What if a wildcard scenario happens tomorrow? What if we can turn a crisis into an opportunity?

Lean In and Enjoy the Ride

As we mentioned in the beginning of the book, life is a rollercoaster: Those who thrive the most are those who enjoy the ride. There are many obstacles faced by small and medium-sized enterprises to enact change to increase their future readiness. Instead of resisting these changes and looking at obstacles as blockers that need to removed, one can ask: *"Why not lean in?"* Lean into emotional appeals to encourage and empower employees to change, lean into positive relationships between leaders and followers to grow together, lean in to understand trends in the environment and a revised understanding of urgency, and lean in to embrace uncertainty. With the right mindset and the right people, SMEs can be unstoppable. The biggest winners are indeed small.

Notes

Part One: Introduction

Chapter 1: Predictably Unpredictable

1. The Organization for Economic Cooperation and Development (OECD). *Entrepreneurship at a Glance: Employment by Enterprise Size*, 2017.

2. World Bank, "Small and Medium Enterprises (SMEs) Finance," n.d. https://www. worldbank.org/en/topic/smefinance.

3. International Labour Organization, "The Power of Small: Unlocking the Potential of SMEs," 2019, https://www.ilo.org/infostories/en-GB/Stories/Employment/ SMEs#power-of-small.

4. McKinsey, "Unlocking Growth in Small and Medium-size Enterprises," July 2, 2020, https://www.mckinsey.com/industries/public-and-social-sector/our-insights/ unlocking-growth-in-small-and-medium-size-enterprises.

5. R. Dai, H. Feng, J. Hu, Q. Jin, H. Li, R. Wang, L. Xu, and X. Zhang. "The Impact of COVID-19 on Small and Medium-sized Enterprises: Evidence from Two-wave Phone Surveys in China," September 2020, Center for Global Development. https://www.cgdev.org/publication/impact-covid-19-small-and-medium-sized-enterprises-evidence-two-wave-phone-surveys-china.

6. Bloomberg Associates, "COVID-19 Economic Impact Analysis: A Summary Report to the Greater London Authority Examining The Economic Impact of COVID-19 on London SMEs," Greater London Authority, August 2020.

7. *CNBC*, "CNBC Disruptor 50," 2020, https://www.cnbc.com/2020/06/16/meet-the-2020-cnbc-disruptor-50-companies.html.

8. *CNBC*, "CNBC Disruptor 50," 2023, https://www.cnbc.com/2023/05/09/these-are-the-2023-cnbc-disruptor-50-companies.html.

Part Two: Understanding Future Readiness

Chapter 2: Nomological Network of Future Readiness

1. R. Rajah, A. de Fauconberg, and O. Woeffray, "Future Readiness of SMEs: Mobilizing the SME Sector to Drive Widespread Sustainability and Prosperity," World Economic Forum, 2021, https://www.weforum.org/whitepapers/future-readiness-of-smes-mobilizing-the-sme-sector-to-drive-widespread-sustainability-and-prosperity/.

2. Levven, "Making Homes More Affordable to Build, Purchase, and Operate," 2023, https://levven.com/.

3. Altron FinTech, "Altron HealthTech Launches Patient-centric Telemedicine Offering with RecoMed," August 17, 2020, https://www.itweb.co.za/content/DZQ587VPA91qzXy2.

4. European Commission, "Climate Action: CO_2 Emission Performance Standards for Cars and Vans," 2020, https://climate.ec.europa.eu/eu-action/transport/road-transport-reducing-co2-emissions-vehicles/co2-emission-performance-standards-cars-and-vans_en#.

5. G. T. Lumpkin and G. G. Dess, "Clarifying the Entrepreneurial Orientation Construct and Linking it to Performance," *Academy of Management Review* 21, no. 1 (1996): 135–172.

6. D. Obstfeld, "Social Networks, the Tertius Iungens Orientation, and Involvement in Innovation," *Administrative Science Quarterly* 50, no. 1 (2005): 100–130.

7. R. S. Burt, *Structural Holes* (Cambridge, MA: Harvard University Press, 1992).

8. M. S. Granovetter, "The Strength of Weak Ties," *American Journal of Sociology* 78, no. 6 (1973): 1360–1380.

9. World Economic Forum, "Measuring Stakeholder Capitalism Towards Common Metrics and Consistent Reporting of Sustainable Value Creation", September 2020, White Paper.

10. B. J. Avolio, W. L. Gardner, F. O. Walumbwa, F. Luthans, and D. R. May, "Unlocking the Mask: A Look at the Process by Which Authentic Leaders Impact Follower Attitudes and Behaviors," *The Leadership Quarterly* 15, no. 6 (2004): 801–823.

11. F. O. Walumbwa, B. J. Avolio, W. L. Gardner, T. S. Wernsing, and S. J. Peterson, "Authentic Leadership: Development and Validation of a Theory-Based Measure," *Journal of Management* 34, no. 1 (2008): 89–126.

12. A. Edmondson, "Psychological Safety and Learning Behavior in Work Teams," *Administrative Science Quarterly* 44, no. 2 (1999): 350–383.

Chapter 3: Global Assessment of the Future Readiness of SMEs

1. A. Haimerl, "Those Businesses That Pivoted During the Pandemic? Some Pivots Became Permanent," *New York Times,* June 8, 2023, https://www.nytimes.com/2023/06/08/business/business-pivoting-covid.html.

2. A. Mueller, S. Anderson, and P. Rathburn, "The Cost of Hiring a New Employee," *Investopedia*, April 8, 2022, https://investopedia.com/financial-edge/0711/the-cost-of-hiring-a-new-employee.aspx.

Part Three: Challenges in the Market Environment

Chapter 4: Sustainability

1. A. Carroll and A. Buchholtz, *Business and Society: Ethics and Stakeholder Management* (Stamford: Cengage Learning, 2003).

2. W. Kenton, "Carbon Credits and How They Can Offset Your Carbon Footprint," *Investopedia*, April 30, 2023, https://www.investopedia.com/terms/c/carbon_credit.asp.

3. R. Rajah and O. Woeffray (eds.), "Future Readiness of SMEs and Mid-Sized Companies: A Year On," World Economic Forum, 2022, https://www.weforum.org/reports/future-readiness-of-smes-and-mid-sized-companies-a-year-on/.

4. *Ibid.*

5. rehyphen, "rehyphen: About," 2023, https://www.rehyphen.org/.

6. Salinda Resort, "The Purple Purpose," 2023, https://salindaresort.com/sustainability/the-purple-purpose.

7. J. McClymont, "What's the Difference? Scope 1, 2 and 3 Corporate Emissions," *Work for Climate*, November 16, 2021, https://www.workforclimate.org/post/whats-the-difference-scope-1-2-and-3-corporate-emissions.

8. *Global Compliance News*, "Singapore: Carbon Pricing (Amendment) Act 2022 Comes Into Force on 7 March 2023," 2022, https://www.globalcompliancenews.com/2023/03/28/https-insightplus-bakermckenzie-com-bm-energy-mining-infrastructure_1-singapore-carbon-pricing-amendment-act-2022-comes-into-force-on-7-march-2023_03242023/.

9. City Developments Limited (CDL), "Integrated Sustainability Report 2023," 2023a, https://cdlsustainability.com/pdf/CDL_ISR_2023.pdf.

10. City Developments Limited (CDL), "Leadership Commitment & Track Record," 2023b, https://cdlsustainability.com/over-20-years-of-value-creation/green-mark-awards/.

11. K. A. Allman and X. Escobar de Nogales, *Impact Investment: A Practical Guide to Investment Process and Social Impact Analysis* (New Jersey: John Wiley & Sons Inc. Wiley Finance Series, 2015).

12. *Ibid.*

13. R. Rajah, A. de Fauconberg, and O. Woeffray, "Future Readiness of SMEs: Mobilizing the SME Sector to Drive Widespread Sustainability and Prosperity," World Economic Forum, 2021, https://www.weforum.org/whitepapers/future-readiness-of-smes-mobilizing-the-sme-sector-to-drive-widespread-sustainability-and-prosperity/.

Chapter 5: Technology

1. Layoffs Tracker, 2023, https://layoffs.fyi/.

2. The Organization for Economic Cooperation and Development (OECD). *Policy Highlights: The Digital Transformation of SMEs*, 2021.

3. World Economic Forum, "Data Unleashed: Empowering Small and Medium Enterprises (SMEs) for Innovation and Success," 2023, https://www.weforum.org/whitepapers/data-unleashed-empowering-small-and-medium-enterprises-smes-for-innovation-and-success/.

4. Data ScienceTech Institute, "The Three Pillars of AI: Symbols, Neurons and Graphs," 2022, https://www.datasciencetech.institute/the-three-pillars-of-ai-symbols-neurons-and-graphs/.

5. CaseGuard, "The Five Basic Components of AI, New Software Development," 2022, https://caseguard.com/articles/the-five-basic-components-of-ai-new-software-development/.

6. G. Press, "54 Predictions About the State of Data in 2021," *Forbes*, December 30, 2020, https://www.forbes.com/sites/gilpress/2021/12/30/54-predictions-about-the-state-of-data-in-2021/?sh=48eb8f8b397d.

7. Grand View Research, "Artificial Intelligence Market Size, Share & Trends Analysis Report by Solution, by Technology (Deep Learning, Machine Learning), by End-use, by Region, and Segment Forecasts, 2023–2030," 2023, https://www.grandviewresearch.com/industry-analysis/artificial-intelligence-ai-market.

8. The Natural Step, "Interface: The Journey of a Lifetime," 2013, https://www.naturalstep.ca/sites/default/files/case_study_interface.pdf.

9. Z. Jiang, "Why Withholding Information at Work Won't Give You an Advantage," *Harvard Business Review*, November 28, 2019, https://hbr.org/2019/11/why-withholding-information-at-work-wont-give-you-an-advantage.

10. J. Schenker, "Mining the Past to Create A Future With Data And AI," *The Innovator*, 2022, https://theinnovator.news/mining-the-past-to-create-a-future-with-data-and-ai/.

11. Allied Digital, "FinoAllied," 2022, https://www.allieddigital.net/in/software-services/finoallied-conhversational-banking-platform/.

12. E. Segal, "Small Businesses are More Frequent Targets of Cyberattacks Than Larger Companies: New Report," *Forbes*, March 16, 2022, https://www.forbes.com/sites/edwardsegal/2022/03/30/cyber-criminals/?sh=46f510152ae5.

13. N. Drager, "Why a Small Business Sees More Cyberattacks Than Bigger Ones," *Quantum Technologies*, July 28, 2022, https://quantumtechnologies.com/small-business-more-cyberattacks/.

14. T. Chamorro-Premuzic, "Human Error Drives Most Cyber Incidents. Could AI Help?" *Harvard Business Review*, May 3, 2023, https://hbr.org/2023/05/human-error-drives-most-cyber-incidents-could-ai-help.

15. World Economic Forum (2023), *Op. cit.*

16. General Data Protection Regulation (GDPR), "Do Consumers Know Their GDPR Data Privacy Rights?" 2020, https://gdpr.eu/consumers-gdpr-data-privacy-rights/.

17. H. Lovells, "Recent Developments in African Data Protection Laws — Outlook for 2023," *Lexology*, 2023, https://www.lexology.com/library/detail.aspx?g=baef72ee-10bd-4eb9-a614-a990c236bb45#.

18. A. Malik, "Facebook is Removing Several Information Fields from Profiles, Including Religious and Political Views," *TechCrunch*, November 18, 2022, https://techcrunch.com/2022/11/17/facebook-removing-profile-information-fields-religious-political-views/?guccounter=1.

19. J. B. Merill, "Liberal, Moderate or Conservative? See How Facebook Labels You," *New York Times*, August 23, 2016, https://www.nytimes.com/2016/08/24/us/politics/facebook-ads-politics.html.

20. B. Perrigo, "What to Know About the TikTok Security Concerns. *Time*, March 23, 2023, https://time.com/6265651/tiktok-security-us/.

21. J. Rosen, "Flawed AI Makes Robots Racist, Sexist," John Hopkins University, June 22, 2022, https://hub.jhu.edu/2022/06/21/flawed-artificial-intelligence-robot-racist-sexist/.

22. M. Bertrand and S. Mullainathan, "Are Emily and Greg More Employable Than Lakisha and Jamal? A Field Experiment on Labor Market Discrimination," National Bureau of Economic Research: Working Paper No. 9873, 2003.

23. P. M. Kline, E. K. Rose, and C. R. Walters, "Systemic Discrimination Among Large U.S. Employers," University of Chicago: Working Paper No. 2021-94, 2021.

24. H.-A. Lee and M. A. Khalid, "High Degrees: Race and Graduate Hiring in Malaysia," *Journal of the Asia Pacific Economy* 21, no. 1 (2016): 53–76.

25. Pulsifi, "Talent Prediction Made Easy," 2022, https://pulsifi.me/.

26. Zapier, "Zapier Report: Marketers Lead the Pack in Automation at Work," July 26, 2021, https://zapier.com/blog/report-marketers-lead-automation-use/.

27. Careera, "Social Responsibility," 2023, https://careera.io/investors.

28. McKinsey, "These 9 Technological Innovations Will Shape the Sustainability Agenda in 2019," 2019, https://www.mckinsey.com/capabilities/sustainability/our-insights/sustainability-blog/these-9-technological-innovations-will-shape-the-sustainability-agenda-in-2019.

29. Kuza, "Revolutionizing Rural Businesses," 2022, https://www.kuza.one/.

30. J. C. Collins and J. I. Porras, "Building Your Company's Vision," *Harvard Business Review* 74 (1996): 65–78.

31. *Ibid.*

Part Four: People as an Asset

Chapter 6: The 3 Rs of Talent: Resourcefulness, Resilience, and Right for the Company

1. HR Shelf, "What is the Actual Cost of Training Employees?" 2022, https://hrshelf.com/cost-of-training-employees/.

2. *Training Magazine*, "2021 Training Industry Report," 2021, https://pubs.royle.com/publication/?m=20617&i=727569&p=20.

3. U.S. Bureau of Labor Statistics, "Job Openings and Labor Turnover Survey: Job Openings and Quits Reach Record Highs in 2021, Layoffs and Discharges Fall to Record Lows," 2022, https://www.bls.gov/opub/mlr/2022/article/job-openings-and-quits-reach-record-highs-in-2021.htm.

4. U.S. Bureau of Labor Statistics, "Job Openings and Labor Turnover Survey: Job Openings Reach Record Highs in 2022 as the Labor Market Recovery Continues," 2023, https://www.bls.gov/opub/mlr/2023/article/job-openings-reach-record-highs-in-2022-as-the-labor-market-recovery-continues.htm.

5. Microsoft, "Work Trend Index Annual Report," 2022, https://www.microsoft.com/en-us/worklab/work-trend-index/great-expectations-making-hybrid-work-work.

6. N. P. Podsakoff, J. A. LePine, and M. A. LePine, "Differential Challenge Stressor-Hindrance Stressor Relationships with Job Attitudes, Turnover Intentions, Turnover, and Withdrawal Behavior: A Meta-Analysis," *Journal of Applied Psychology* 92, no. 2 (2007): 438.

7. R. D. Zimmerman and T. C. Darnold, "The Impact of Job Performance on Employee Turnover Intentions and the Voluntary Turnover Process: A Meta-Analysis and Path Model," *Personnel Review* 38, no. 2 (2009): 142–158.

8. Gallup, "State of the American Workplace," 2023, https://www.gallup.com/workplace/349484/state-of-the-global-workplace.aspx.

9. J. Moss, "Burnout is About Your Workplace, Not Your People," *Harvard Business Review,* 2019, https://hbr.org/2019/12/burnout-is-about-your-workplace-not-your-people.

10. Centers for Disease Control and Prevention, D. M. Stone, K. A. Mack, and J. Qualters, "Notes from the Field: Recent Changes in Suicide Rates, by Race and Ethnicity and Age Group — United States, 2021," *Morbidity and Mortality Weekly Report* 72, no. 6 (2023): 160–162. http://dx.doi.org/10.15585/mmwr.mm7206a4.

11. *Channel NewsAsia,* "476 Suicides Reported in Singapore in 2022; Highest in More Than 20 Years," July 1, 2023, https://www.channelnewsasia.com/singapore/suicides-reported-singapore-476-2022-highest-more-20-years-3597791.

12. Samaritans of Singapore, "Learn About Suicide: The Quick Facts," 2023, https://www.sos.org.sg/learn-about-suicide/quick-facts.

13. J. Fuller and W. Kerr, "The Great Resignation Didn't Start with the Pandemic," *Harvard Business Review,* 2022, https://hbr.org/2022/03/the-great-resignation-didnt-start-with-the-pandemic.

14. World Economic Forum, "The Future of Jobs Report 2023," 2023, https://www.weforum.org/publications/the-future-of-jobs-report-2023/.

15. Glints, "Southeast Asia Startup Talent Report 2023," 2023, https://employers.glints.sg/ebooks/southeast-asia-startup-talent-report-2023.

16. Glassdoor, "Sharesource Interview Questions," 2023, https://www.glassdoor.com/Interview/Sharesource-Interview-Questions-E2322690.htm.

17. *Ibid.*

18. Sharesource, "About Us," 2023, https://www.sharesource.com.au/about-us.

19. R. Greene and N. Conrad, "Basic Assumptions and Terms," in *Resiliency: An Integrated Approach to Practice, Policy, and Research,* ed. R. Greene (Washington, DC: National Association of Social Workers Press, 2002): 1–27.

20. N. N. Taleb, *Antifragile: Things that Gain from Disorder* (New York: Random House, 2012).

21. R. Rajah and R. D. Arvey, "Helping Group Members Develop Resilience," in *Handbook of Research on Crisis Leadership in Organizations,* ed. A. J. Dubrin (Northampton, MA: Edward Elgar Publishing, 2013): 149–173.

22. B. L. Fredrickson, "The Broaden–and–Build Theory of Positive Emotions." *Philosophical Transactions of the Royal Society of London. Series B: Biological Sciences* 359, no. 1449 (2004): 1367–1377.

23. A. S. Masten, "Ordinary Magic: Resilience Processes in Development". *American Psychologist* 56, no. 3 (2001): 227–238.

24. F. Luthans, G. R. Vogelgesang, and P. B. Lester, "Developing the Psychological Capital of Resiliency", *Human Resource Development Review* 5, no. 1 (2006): 25–44.

25. A. Edmondson, "Psychological Safety and Learning Behavior in Work Teams," *Administrative Science Quarterly* 44, no. 2 (1999): 350–383.

26. Gallup, "State of the American Workplace," 2017, https://www.gallup.com/workplace/238085/state-american-workplace-report-2017.aspx.

27. R. Rajah and O. Woeffray (eds.), "Future Readiness of SMEs and Mid-Sized Companies: A Year On," World Economic Forum, 2022, https://www.weforum.org/reports/future-readiness-of-smes-and-mid-sized-companies-a-year-on/.

28. C. A. O'Reilly, J. Chatman, and D. F. Caldwell, "People and Organizational Culture: A Profile Comparison Approach to Assessing Person-Organization Fit," *Academy of Management Journal* 34, no. 3 (1991): 487–515.

29. N. Granados and A. Gupta, "Transparency Strategy: Competing with Information in a Digital World," *MIS Quarterly* 37, no. 2 (2013): 5–9. (Special Issue: Digital Business Strategy).

Chapter 7: Leadership

1. J. Vergauwe, B. Wille, J. Hofmans, R. B. Kaiser, and F. De Fruyt, "The Double-Edged Sword of Leader Charisma: Understanding the Curvilinear Relationship between Charismatic Personality and Leader Effectiveness," *Journal of Personality and Social Psychology* 114, no. 1 (2018): 110–130.

2. J. C. Collins and J. I. Porras, "Organizational Vision and Visionary Organizations," *California Management Review* 34, no. 1 (1991): 30–52.

3. R. Rajah and R. D. Arvey, "Helping Group Members Develop Resilience," in *Handbook of Research on Crisis Leadership in Organizations*, ed. A. J. Dubrin (Northampton, MA: Edward Elgar Publishing, 2013): 149–173.

4. R. Rajah, Z. Song, and R. D. Arvey, "Emotionality and Leadership: Taking Stock of the Past Decade of Research," *The Leadership Quarterly 22, no. 6* (2011): 1107–1119.

5. F. W. Taylor, *Principles of Scientific Management* (Westport, CT: Greenwood Press Publishers, 1972) (originally written 1909).

6. B. M. Bass and B. J. Avolio, "Transformational Leadership and Organizational Culture," *Public Administration Quarterly 17* (1993): 112–121.

7. L. G. Bolman and T. E. Deal, "Leadership and Management Effectiveness: A Multi-Frame, Multi-Sector Analysis," *Human Resource Management 30*, no. 4 (1991): 509–534.

8. L. G. Bolman and T. E. Deal, *Reframing Organizations: Artistry, Choice, and Leadership* (7th edn.) (San Francisco: Jossey-Bass, 2021).

9. Rajah *et al.* (2011), *Op. cit.*

10. F. O. Walumbwa, B. J. Avolio, W. L. Gardner, T. S. Wernsing, and S. J. Peterson, "Authentic Leadership: Development and Validation of a Theory-Based Measure," *Journal of Management 34*, no. 1 (2008): 89–126.

11. M. J. Newcombe and N. M. Ashkanasy, "The Role of Affect and Affective Congruence in Perceptions of Leaders: An Experimental Study," *The Leadership Quarterly 13*, no. 5 (2002): 601–614.

12. H. Ibarra, "The Authenticity Paradox," *Harvard Business Review 93* (2015): 53–59.

13. J. Reb, J. Narayanan, and S. Chaturvedi, "Leading Mindfully: Two Studies on the Influence of Supervisor Trait Mindfulness on Employee Well-Being and Performance," *Mindfulness 5*, no. 1 (2014): 36–45.

14. K. Parker and J. M. Horowitz, "Majority of Workers Who Quit a Job in 2021 Cite Low Pay, no Opportunities for Advancement, Feeling Disrespected," *Pew Research Center*, March 9, 2022, https://www.pewresearch.org/short-reads/2022/03/09/majority-of-workers-who-quit-a-job-in-2021-cite-low-pay-no-opportunities-for-advancement-feeling-disrespected/.

15. B. George, *Discover Your True North* (Hoboken: John Wiley & Sons, 2015).

16. S. Jackson, "Nvidia's CEO Gave a Super Honest Account of What It's Like to Start Your Own Business. It Should Be Required Reading for Anyone

Considering It," *Business Insider,* October 22, 2023, https://www.businessinsider.com/nvidia-ceo-jensen-huang-comments-how-hard-starting-own-business-2023-10.

Part Five: Change Management

Chapter 8: Just Pivot

1. C. Christensen, *The Innovator's Dilemma: When New Technologies Cause Great Firms to Fail* (Boston: Harvard Business Review Press, 1997).

2. D. K. Rigby and A. Corbett, "It Takes Systems, Not Serendipity: A Blueprint for Building a Disruptive-Innovation Engine," *Ivey Business Journal* 67, no. 2 (2002): 189–208.

3. Arizona State University, "Disruptive Innovation and the Business Models that Make Them Successful," June 22, 2021, https://thunderbird.asu.edu/thought-leadership/insights/disruptive-innovation-and-business-models-make-them-successful.

4. W. Weitzel and E. Jonsson, "Decline in Organizations: A Literature Integration and Extension," *Administrative Science Quarterly* 34, no. 1 (1989): 91–109.

5. J. D. Thompson, *Organizations in Action* (New York: McGraw-Hill, 1967).

6. W. Shih, "The Real Lessons from Kodak's Decline," *MIT Sloan Management Review* 57, no. 4 (2016): 11–13.

7. *Ibid.*

8. *Ibid.*

9. P. Andrews, "Heavyweights Go Toe to Toe: Microsoft Internet Explorer vs. Netscape Navigator," *The Seattle Times,* 1996, August 25, http://community.seattletimes.nwsource.com/archive/?date=19960825&slug=2345940.

10. R. Rajah and R. D. Arvey, "Helping Group Members Develop Resilience," in *Handbook of Research on Crisis Leadership in Organizations,* ed. A. J. Dubrin (Northampton, MA: Edward Elgar Publishing, 2013): 149–173.

11. Accenture, "U.S. Companies Losing Customers as Consumers Demand More Human Interaction, Accenture Strategy Study Finds," March 23, 2016, https://newsroom.accenture.com/news/us-companies-losing-customers-as-consumers-demand-more-human-interaction-accenture-strategy-study-finds.htm.

12. CGS, "CGS Survey Reveals Consumers Prefer a Hybrid AI/Human Approach to Customer Service. Is There Chatbot Fatigue?" 2019, https://www.cgsinc.com/en/resources/2019-CGS-Customer-Service-Chatbots-Channels-Survey.

13. Y. Ruan and J. Mezei, "When Do AI Chatbots Lead to Higher Customer Satisfaction than Human Frontline Employees in Online Shopping Assistance? Considering Product Attribute Type," *Journal of Retailing and Consumer Services* 68 (2022): 103059.

14. T. Brown, "Design Thinking," *Harvard Business Review* 86, no. 6 (2008): 84–92.

15. H. Boyd, S. McKernon, B. Mullin, and A. Old, "Improving Healthcare Through the Use of Co-design," *New Zealand Medical Journal* 125, no. 1357 (2012): 4–15.

16. J. Kotter, "Leading Change: Why Transformation Efforts Fail," *Harvard Business Review* 73, no. 2 (1995): 55–67.

17. K. Piper, "The Case Against Colonizing Space to Save Humanity," *Vox*, October 22, 2018.

18. K. Lewin, *Field Theory in Social Sciences* (New York: Harper & Row, 1947).

19. L. V. Gerstner, *Who says Elephants can't Dance?: Leading a Great Enterprise Through Dramatic Change* (New York: HarperBusiness, 2009).

20. Ayce Labor y Tax, "SME vs. Family Business: Where are the Differences?," September 15, 2021, https://www.aycelaborytax.com/en/blog/sme-vs-family-business-where-are-the-differences/.

21. A. Logan and A. Desai, *The State of the Nation: The UK Family Business Sector 2019–20* (UK: IFB Research Foundation, 2020).

22. B. Sarkar, "More Family Businesses in Asia Now Paying Attention to Leadership Succession: Report," *The Economic Times,* November 10, 2021.

23. J. Hoomans, "35,000 Decisions: The Great Choices of Strategic Leaders," *Roberts Wesleyan University: The Leading Edge*, March 20, 2015, https://go.roberts.edu/leadingedge/the-great-choices-of-strategic-leaders.

24. Hawksford, "How to Overcome Succession Planning Challenges in Family-owned Businesses, April 6, 2023, https://www.hawksford.com/insights-and-guides/family-business-succession-planning.

25. Consultancy.asia, "Leadership Succession Challenges for Asian Family Businesses," January 31, 2022, https://www.consultancy.asia/news/4672/leadership-succession-challenges-for-asian-family-businesses.

26. PricewaterhouseCoopers, "10th Global Family Business Survey," 2021, https://www.pwc.com/gx/en/family-business-services/family-business-survey-2021/pwc-family-business-survey-2021.pdf.

27. S. Denning, "How to Make the Whole Organization 'Agile,'" *Strategy & Leadership* 44, no. 4 (2016): 10–17.

28. PALO IT, "PALO IT Works with CIX to Seize More Green Growth Opportunities," June 16, 2023, https://blog.palo-it.com/en/palo-it-works-with-cix-to-seize-more-green-growth-opportunities.

29. Gerstner (2009), *Op. cit.*

30. O. Woeffray and P. Carvalho, "The Future Isn't What It Used to Be: Here's How Strategic Foresight Can Help," World Economic Forum, February 6, 2023, https://www.weforum.org/agenda/2023/02/strategic-intelligence-why-foresight-key-future-readiness/.

Index

Printed in the United States
by Baker & Taylor Publisher Services